MORE MONEY NOW

MORE MONEY NOW

USE YOUR EXISTING SKILLS, CONNECTIONS AND TECHNOLOGY TO START EARNING CASH TODAY

MICHAEL ZECHMANN

NEW YORK

NASHVILLE • MELBOURNE • VANCOUVER

MORE MONEY NOW

Use Your Existing Skills, Connections and Technology to Start Earning Cash Today

Published in New York, New York, by Morgan James Publishing. Morgan James is a trademark of Morgan James, LLC. www.MorganJamesPublishing.com

The Morgan James Speakers Group can bring authors to your live event. For more information or to book an event visit The Morgan James Speakers Group at www.TheMorganJamesSpeakersGroup.com.

ISBN 9781683504627 paperback
ISBN 9781683504634 eBook
Library of Congress Control Number: 2017902309

Cover Design and Interior Design by:
Chris Treccani
www.3dogcreative.net

In an effort to support local communities, raise awareness and funds, Morgan James Publishing donates a percentage of all book sales for the life of each book to Habitat for Humanity Peninsula and Greater Williamsburg.

Get involved today! Visit
www.MorganJamesBuilds.com

DEDICATION

For Rebeca, Catherine, and Madeline, who are the
inspiration and the reason for everything.

EPIGRAPH

An investment in knowledge pays the best interest.
–Benjamin Franklin

Screw it, let's do it!
–Richard Branson

TABLE OF CONTENTS

Introduction   *xi*

LAYING THE FOUNDATION FOR SUCCESS   1
Chapter 1:   A Changing Landscape   3
Chapter 2:   Avoiding Scams   13
Chapter 3:   Know Thyself   19

PROVIDING SERVICES FROM HOME   29
Chapter 4:   Being a Remote Worker—   31
                An Overview and Some Starting Points
Chapter 5:   Freelance Writing   45
Chapter 6:   A Few More Work-from-Home   61
                Opportunities

PROVIDING SERVICES IN YOUR COMMUNITY   73
Chapter 7:   Driving for Dollars   75
Chapter 8:   Caregiving   83
Chapter 9:   More Services You Can Provide   95
                Around Town

SELLING GOODS   105

Chapter 10:   Selling Online   107
Chapter 11:   Selling in Your Community   119

ADDITIONAL INTERESTING GIGS   129
Chapter 12:   Becoming Part of the Crowd   131
Chapter 13:   Unconventional Money-Makers   139

Conclusion   *147*
About the Author   *149*

INTRODUCTION

I'm not much of a gambler, but I'd be willing to bet that the vast majority of us would like to have more money than we have right now. It doesn't matter whether we'd use the extra money for daily living, paying off a debt or saving up for a dream vacation. It doesn't matter if we're a college student, a 30-something parent with a full-time job, or a retiree living on a fixed income. The one thing we have in common is that we wish we had more cash in our pockets.

So we keep on dreaming about how great that would feel, and we keep on praying that our ship comes in before the dock rots. But we don't take any concrete steps to make our dream a reality (other than buying our weekly lottery tickets and crossing our fingers, that is). Perhaps that's because we don't really believe it can happen for us. We are afraid we don't have the right skills or enough time to invest in a money-making venture. Or we do have skills and time but we don't know where to start.

I've met far too many people who are struggling to make ends meet these days, and the way the economy's going it may get worse before it gets better. Obamacare has caused businesses to cut their workers' hours as a cost-saving measure, and the employees and their families are being forced to get by with smaller paychecks. The cost of college tuition has skyrocketed, putting graduates in a deep pit of student loan debt—an average of $35,000[1]—before they even have a chance to earn a dime as members of the workforce. Not only that, but their prospects of finding a job immediately out of college are slim: just 14-percent of new grads managed to land a career-type job in 2015.[2]

The stats aren't much better for their parents and grandparents. Ten thousand baby boomers are hitting retirement age *every single day*, a trend that will continue until 2030. Whereas life expectancy at birth in 1930 was only 58-years for men and 62 for women, current life expectancy at birth is 78. Full retirement age is 70, but the average retirement age in the United States is still 62.[3] The average retirement length has gone from 13 to 20-years. The fastest growing age bracket percentage-wise is people in their 90s, and that will likely switch to people in their 100s by the year 2020. That means that there will be many 40- and 50-year long retirements. Longer life expectancy means these folks will have to make their retirement income stretch farther than ever before, putting them at risk of running out of money before they run out of years. That's the bad news.

The good news is that I've also met a lot of people—students, retirees, parents of young children and those with kids in college—who have cracked the code and come up with really

1   http://dailycaller.com/2015/05/15/just-14-percent-of-this-years-college-grads-have-real-jobs-waiting/, accessed June 20, 2016.
2   Ibid.
3   https://www.nia.nih.gov/health/publication/growing-older-america-health-and-retirement-study/chapter-2-work-and-retirement

interesting ways to supplement their incomes to meet their challenges. Their stories have inspired me so much that I want to share them with as many people as I can. And that's why I wrote this book.

The truth is, it's never been easier to find something you like to do and make money doing it, whether you've got an hour to spare or whether you're looking to fill a whole day or a 40-hour week. There are unlimited avenues to do that now, and you don't have to start from zero. I've done the research and compiled the stories of people who have figured it out so you can use their experiences as a catalyst for developing your own way forward. By the time you finish reading this book, I promise that you will be inspired by at least one idea for how to make money doing something you enjoy, and you'll have the step-by-step directions for getting started.

Regardless of your age or situation, there is something of value for you in the pages that follow. If you're a student, you could probably use extra money for school and living expenses. You likely have some spare time and newly acquired skills you'd like to practice. If so, this book is for you. It's also for you if you already have a full-time job but are looking for something extra for three to five hours a week. It's for you if you are a stay-at-home mom whose kids go to day care a couple of times a week, but you can't commit to a full-time or even a traditional part-time position. It's also for the person who lives in a rural area and can't find a job to match their skills. This book will guide you toward working remotely, just as if you were in the big city… but without the commute.

And if you're a retiree needing to make your fixed income go further or someone planning for retirement, this book is also for you. It's understandable that you want to live it up in your early years of retirement by traveling or experiencing things you haven't gotten to do before. This book will help you find ways to supplement your income to help you afford these experiences. Not only will you learn about new developments in the marketplace and exciting innovative technologies, but you'll also discover interesting and fulfilling ways to spend your time.

This is important, because recent studies show that the longer we stay engaged in the world around us, the healthier we are. A 2014 study by Chicago's Rush University found that older people can lower their risk of health problems like stroke and dementia simply by living "a life of purpose." Working and volunteering can help you live purposefully. You'll find a slew of ideas for bringing meaning to your life in the chapters ahead.

And if you're a person who's out of work or between jobs and trying to make ends meet, this book is for you, too. It's also for parents who are helping put their kids through college. It's for folks who are saving up to start a business or retire early, and it's for families trying to pay off a debt or create a savings buffer.

Do you feel like you're drifting in a sea of expenses and can't seem to get ahead? What if I told you that all you had to do to pull yourself out of it is to spend a few hours a week doing something you like? Would you do it?

In the chapters ahead, you'll read about:

- How technology and the workplace have changed, making it easier than ever to earn money on the side
- How to identify the type of money-making opportunities that best fit your personality, passion, skills and lifestyle
- Ways to identify and avoid scams
- Interesting stories of people just like you who are making money doing what they love
- Dozens of real ways to earn money by selling goods and/or providing services from your home and in your community
- And much more

Whoever you are and whatever your situation, this book will show you the steps you can take to secure your financial future, declare your freedom from debt and accomplish your goals. And you don't have to win a multi-million dollar lottery jackpot to do it. It doesn't require an enormous windfall to start positively impacting your finances. Just ask any millionaire and they'll tell you it's true. Most affluent people in the United States today became that way simply by knowing how much money was coming in and how much was going out, and always choosing to save at least ten percent of their income. I recognize that's a struggle for many people, but by reading this book you can find ways to increase your earning potential little by little without finding a new job or switching careers.

For example, if you could bring in just $500 more per month and save it, over ten years you would have in your bank account $79,084 (assuming a six percent growth rate). If you could keep that up for 20 years, you'd have accumulated $220,713. That would definitely help make retirement more comfortable, wouldn't it?

The same principle applies to credit card debt. Let's say you owe $50,000 on a credit card with an interest rate of 23.99 percent. Paying an extra $500 a month on that bill would have you debt free in about five years. Imagine having that kind of freedom… and all it took was an additional $500 a month!

Everyone wants to get ahead financially, but few people recognize the opportunities that are all around them. This book provides you with a road map for finding and seizing those opportunities. Most of them are not time-intensive to get involved with. In fact, you can try many of them for three or four hours just to test the waters without making a huge commitment of time or energy. And you don't have to be a computer wiz to do many of these activities. To help you out, I've graded each one on a "tech savvy" scale of 1 to 5. Activities with a ranking of 1 require little to no knowledge of technology and those with a ranking of 5 require extensive knowledge (such as freelance computer programming, for example). Everything else falls somewhere in between.

So let's dive in and get started on our search for the perfect money-making opportunity for you.

LAYING THE FOUNDATION FOR SUCCESS

CHAPTER 1:

A CHANGING LANDSCAPE

Not so long ago, the options for bringing in extra cash were pretty limited. You could get a part-time job working for a local business. You could peddle products for companies like Avon, Tupperware, Fuller Brush and Amway, or you could sell some of your own stuff at a yard sale, consignment store or pawn shop. You could take on odd jobs such as detailing cars, babysitting, painting houses, or mowing lawns. To find these kinds of gigs you'd read the want ads in the daily newspaper and ask around town to see if anyone needed help. Your choices were restricted by conventionality and geography. You could do only what your local market and the people around you would accept, and the work had to be close to where you lived.

But things are different today. Technology has disrupted entire industries and effected the way business is conducted, forcing people to adapt to the changes or be left behind. The online transportation network Uber has put many taxi drivers out of business while giving the rest of us the chance to moonlight as self-employed chauffeurs. Angieslist.com has changed how service businesses market themselves... and how customers express their feelings about those services. Amazon.com has hurt retail stores, which have always been a major source of employment for high school and college students and people in their later years looking to supplement their retirement incomes. AirBnB.com and VRBO.com have made it possible for individual property owners to essentially become hoteliers or vacation rental managers. Freelancing and virtual workplaces have changed the temp worker landscape. Care.com has transformed the way people connect with and hire professional caregivers.

As these examples show, we're no longer restricted by tradition and location when it comes to making money on the side (or even on a full-time basis). Attitudes about telecommuting have shifted so much that nowadays you can work from home for a boss sitting half way around the world and nobody is surprised by that. Because of modern technology, you don't have to spend a lot of time learning additional skills unless you want to; you can leverage the expertise you've already accumulated and apply it to something new. You have the freedom to try a lot of different things without making a major time commitment to any one of them. The possibilities are endless. You can pick when and where you want to work, and choose how many hours you want to devote. It doesn't matter how young or old you are. You're free to pursue something you're passionate about and see if you can make it pay off.

Let me tell you a story that illustrates my point. "Jeanette" is a widow in her early 70s who lives in a part of the country known for its scenic beauty. After Jeanette's husband passed away a few years ago, she renewed her interest in wildlife photography as an outlet for dealing with her grief. She also wanted to get active again following some minor surgery, so she started kayaking around her island shooting pictures of marine life, birds of prey and shorebirds. She enlarged and framed several of her favorite photos and hung them on the wall in her house.

One evening Jeanette hosted a dinner party at her home, and a guest admired one of her photographs of a soaring red-tailed hawk. She asked Jeanette if she could buy it for her granddaughter, whose bedroom was decorated in a wildlife theme. Flattered, Jeanette agreed to sell the picture. Also at the dinner party was a member of Jeanette's church who owned a gift shop. He encouraged Jeanette to make blank greeting cards with her photos on the front so he could sell them to tourists at his shop. Jeanette did so. Much to her surprise the cards sold out in a matter of days. Jeanette summoned the courage to approach another gift shop owner on a neighboring island who also agreed to sell the cards. It wasn't long before Jeanette's little cards were available practically everywhere—even in the region's major grocery and drug store chains. She had to hire a high school art student to help her make cards so she could keep up with the demand.

A few weeks later there was to be a big art festival, one of the highlights of peak tourist season in the area. Jeanette took a deep breath, signed up as an exhibitor and paid the entry fee. She and her young assistant made a huge batch of greeting cards to take to the show. She also enlarged and framed some of her best photographs to offer for sale.

I'm happy to report that Jeanette's booth was a huge hit. She made several thousand dollars at that first show. As it turns out, the windfall came just in the nick of time. Unfortunately Jeanette was not prepared for the adverse affect her husband's death would have on her taxes. The proceeds from the art festival helped her meet her tax obligations the first year after her husband's passing.

Since then Jeanette has become one of the area's most prolific wildlife photographers. Not only does she enjoy fantastic health due to all the exercise she gets paddling her kayak around the island taking pictures, but she's also making thousands of dollars a year. Last tourist season she earned enough to take her grandkids on a cruise, purchase a better lens for her camera and buy some new photo editing software, which she is learning to use through an online class. Her tech-savvy assistant also helped her set up a website that serves as a virtual storefront where she sells her photographs to buyers all around the world.

It would have been impossible for Jeanette to achieve success this way just 20 years ago. But because she was willing to evolve and harness the power of today's technology, she was able to carve out an exciting new way forward by engaging in a fun activity that also supplements her retirement income. Jeanette's story proves that when you follow your passion, have an open mind and the courage to take risks, you can attain fulfillment doing something you love *and* make money at the same time.

It's never been easier to find creative ways to make money, but you have to remember that this isn't your grandpa's job hunt. The traditional job search—reading "help wanted" ads, attending job fairs (also known as career expos), and/or signing up with a temp agency–simply won't give you full access to the incredible array of opportunities that are out there waiting for you. There are countless apps and other cutting-edge technologies that make it possible for you to connect directly with clients, employers and consumers… 24-hours a day, seven days a week, no matter how many time zones separate you.

Here's a great example of that: I was listening to the radio during my commute the other day when I heard a story about a website called NaTakallam.com, which is Arabic for "We Speak." NaTakallam connects students from all around the world who want to learn conversational Arabic with tutors who happen to be Syrian refugees living in Lebanon. The tutors, many of whom worked as doctors, lawyers and educators in their homeland, are now living in poverty because they are barred from getting jobs in Lebanon until they get a work permit. After being trained by NaTakallam staff, the tutors take a laptop computer, go to a Wi-Fi hotspot near their refugee camps and meet one-on-one with their students via Skype. They practice speaking Arabic together for an hour, after which the student uses the NaTakallam website to pay the tutor $15 per session. Ten dollars goes to the tutor and $5 goes to NaTakallam so they can maintain the technology and keep on training new tutors. This service is a huge help for the tutor and a genuinely enlightening experience for the student. The tutors—who have gone from being helpless victims of war to self-employed entrepreneurs—are now empowered to work as many hours a week as they want.

See, this is what I'm talking about. What a great example of how modern technology and changing views about work have merged to open more and more doors for people. You'd never find an opportunity like that in your local newspaper. It's true that the classified ad section of the daily paper is still a good resource for finding full-time jobs within your community. It's easy to use, inexpensive, or in some cases, free. It gives you quick access to a wide variety of opportunities (depending on where you live, of course. Urban areas tend to have more robust classified ads than rural areas.) But the classifieds are not necessarily intended for people who are wanting to moonlight or find interesting ways to supplement their income. Neither are the online job boards like CareerBuilder.com, Monster.com, LiveCareer.com, etc. Again, these are mostly for the traditional full-time job hunter. So too are career fairs, which have always been considered a time saver since they get you in front of a lot of potential employers at once; plus they're free to attend. But they're not the best use of your energy if you're only looking to earn some extra income or fill up your free time. The same applies to registering with the standard temp agencies like Manpower, Adecco and Kelly. They can connect you with a job but probably not one that gives you the freedom to choose when, where, and how much you'll work.

In my mind the best way to drum up those kinds of money-making opportunities is through a combination of modern technology and good old-fashioned networking. I want to devote some time to a discussion of networking here, because it's really important.

The Power of Your Network

Networking has gotten a bad rap over the years, and I think that's because people are confused about what it really is. Networking isn't about mingling and trading business cards with a bunch of strangers during an awkward cocktail hour in a hotel meeting room. It's not about tooting your own horn or schmoozing for favors. It's not about using people. It's about being open and curious. It's about being generous with your time and your resources. In essence, it's about doing something you already know how to do: developing relationships.

And what is at the core of relationship development? Give and take. Human beings are wired to help one another. We crave meaningful connection. So it's a safe bet that the people around you want to connect with you and help you, and that you want to do the same for them. Therefore, if you can think of networking as simply *developing new connections and strengthening old ones via mutual give and take*, it's not nearly as intimidating or mysterious.

To get started, make a list of all the people you know— your family members; friends; current and former classmates, colleagues, bosses and clients; acquaintances; neighbors; teachers; coaches; people with whom you worship; your dentist; your mail carrier… and onward you go. These are the people in your network right now. Write down their names. Check your email contacts, social media accounts and address book to see if there's anyone you've missed. You'll probably be surprised by how large your network actually is.

◆

Consider each person in your network as a potentially powerful link to a new source of opportunities.

◆

Next, identify exactly what it is you hope to achieve by tapping into your network. This is one of those times when it's best to be explicit. Issuing a vague appeal for everybody to be on the lookout for a generic opportunity will not get you as far as will being specific. Therefore you're not going to tell the people in your network that you're *looking for ways to make a little extra money.* You're going to tell them that you are wanting to *do bookkeeping for small- to medium-sized businesses.*

Now you can begin contacting the folks in your network. Start with those closest to you and work your way outward from there. As you initiate these contacts, always keep it front and center in your mind that the purpose of this activity is to develop and strengthen your relationships. Getting job tips and referrals is only a happy by-product of that. Above all else, be gracious and authentic in your communications. Launch each conversation by connecting with the person. How have they and their family been? What's new and interesting in their world? Listen carefully because they may say something that presents you with an opportunity to offer them assistance, or at the very least, some encouragement. When the conversation turns to your search for work, remember to be specific about what it is you're looking for. To expand your network, ask if they can think of anyone else you should talk to about this. Also ask if they have any advice for you. People love to give advice… just ask your mom (or mine). Before you let the person go, be sure to thank them for visiting with you and encourage them to reach out to you whenever they want.

Your contact has now given you the gift of their time and attention. Since this is a mutually-beneficial relationship you're trying to nurture, how might you reciprocate? You could write them a thank-you note. You could check in with them in a few weeks just to see how they're doing. If you read an interesting article you think they might enjoy, you can clip it and send it to them (or email the link if it's online). Or if you hear about an opportunity that's perfect for them, you can call and give them a heads up.

That's all there is to networking. That's not so hard after all!

Before we close out this chapter, I want to mention one more resource for finding money-making opportunities, and that's America's most popular classified ad website, **Craigslist. org**. Craigslist operates region-specific sites all around the world and features a variety of traditional classified ad categories including jobs, services, for sale, items wanted, housing, and personals. It also has a category called "gigs" for people looking for short-term engagements in fields like writing, graphic arts and computer services. And if you happen to be an exotic dancer, aspiring "gentleman's companion" or lingerie model, the gigs category is also for you. Craigslist is free to use for job seekers. You simply click through the ads and respond to the ones you like directly through the website.

The good thing about Craigslist is that you can find everything under the sun there. In fact, I know of many people who have snagged decent and interesting work opportunities via that forum. The bad thing about Craigslist is that it has everything under the sun, and I know of people who have been ripped off via that forum.

Which brings us to...

CHAPTER 2:

AVOIDING SCAMS

For all the legitimate money-making opportunities in the world today, there are also a regrettably large number of scams designed to take advantage of innocent people's dreams and, in some cases, their desperation. You must be on your guard, especially if you're going to conduct business or pursue prospects in the largely anonymous world of cyberspace.

One of the most common rip-off schemes involves getting access to an unsuspecting person's bank account information, social security number and other personal identifiers and opening credit accounts in their name without their knowledge or consent. Another is giving the victim a check that represents an overpayment for an item or a service the victim has provided (or is supposed to provide in the future). The victim deposits the check, refunds the overpayment, and finds out a few days later that the check was a fake. Yet another scam requires the victim to pay up front for "necessary" training or items to do the job… and then the training or items never materialize or are substandard in some way.

Here are a few ways you can try to protect yourself from these and similar swindles:

- Beware of opportunities that offer big pay in exchange for little work. Remember the old adage: if it seems too good to be true, it probably is.

- When contacted by a job prospect via email, check the name of the company and the email address carefully. Scammers will often mimic a legitimate company's name by changing a letter here or adding a hyphen there to try to fool you into thinking you're hearing from the real deal. For example, you might think you're getting an exciting offer from Human Resources at Procter & Gamble, but if the signature line says Procter & *Gambel*, trust me… you're not.

- Be wary of emails alleged to come from recognized companies if they end in gmail.com, yahoo.com or other generic domains. Real companies have their own domains, such as IBM.com, Apple.com, Microsoft. com, etc., and their real employees will have email addresses that reflect that.

- Research the people and companies you come in contact with. Do an internet search for the person/company name followed by "scam" and/or "complaints" and see if any results turn up. If they've ripped off other people, it's likely that their past victims have posted the news online somewhere. Also call your local Better Business Bureau or run the company through the Better Business Bureau's website at www.bbb.org.

- Don't pay money up front for anything unless you are opening a franchise, and even then be sure to check out the person and the franchise thoroughly before handing over any funds.

But perhaps the best scam detector you've got is your intuition. If you have the slightest apprehension about a person or an opportunity, walk away. Always, always trust your gut.

The Story of Alisha, a Cautionary Tale...

Like many of today's young parents, "John and Alisha Smith" were struggling to make ends meet. With three children under the age of five, they decided that it made the most sense for John to continue his career in sales while Alisha stayed home with the kids. The cost of child care for three little ones was astronomical in their town. If Alisha were to work outside the home, almost her entire paycheck would go to the day care center.

Alisha took great pride in her role as a stay-at-home mom. She loved being with her kids and firmly believed she was doing the right thing for her family. It was tough though. John was a good salesman but his pay was commission-based, so some months were better than others. Consequently Alisha became a pro at penny pinching. She was a world-class coupon clipper, barterer and buyer-in-bulk. But despite the Smith's best efforts, they were barely squeaking by.

There was one particularly difficult stretch when John's sales took a nose dive. The twins' birthdays were coming up too, and Alisha was really worried. She didn't want to alarm John but she was pretty sure they weren't going to be able to pay their credit card balance that month, let alone give the kids a proper birthday bash in a few weeks. *What in the world are we going to do?*, Alisha thought to herself as she and the kids walked home from the park one chilly afternoon. *I have to find a way to help John bring in more money, and fast.*

Just then she saw a bright yellow flyer stuck to a telephone pole on the corner near their house:

MAKE MONEY AT HOME!
CALL 555-123-4567

Alisha grabbed the flyer off the pole and jammed it into a pocket on the baby's stroller.

"Let's go, kids," Alisha said. "Mommy's got a phone call to make!"

When Alisha got home and called the number on the flyer, she was immediately routed to voicemail. She left a message. A few minutes later a nice woman called her back and explained that the job was assembling jewelry—bracelets, to be exact. The company would send Alisha all the materials she needed to make the items. They'd also send her a training video and a sample bracelet for reference purposes. Alisha would make the pieces in the comfort of her own home and then send them to the company, which would buy each one that met their specifications.

Alisha was thrilled. She was great at crafts. This was right up her alley!

The woman went on to explain that Alisha would need to purchase a "starter kit" for $149.95. The kit contained the sample bracelet, the training video and enough materials to make $300 worth of bracelets.

"That's quite an opportunity, don't you agree?" the woman said. "You can double your money in no time!"

Alisha ordered her starter kit on the spot, charging it to the credit card. She even paid a few dollars extra for rush shipping so she could get started right away.

The kit arrived as promised a few days later. Alisha set up a desk in the corner of the dining room to serve as her little work area. After tucking the kids into bed, she watched the training video. It seemed to leave out a couple of steps in the assembly process, but Alisha was sure she could figure it out as she went along. Eager to begin, she started putting together her first bracelet. Her enthusiasm was quickly replaced with frustration. The wires kept breaking; they didn't bend the way they did in the video, and the holes in some of the the beads were too small to thread onto the wires. In fact, all the materials in the starter kit seemed of lesser quality than those that had gone into the sample bracelet. But Alisha soldiered on.

You can probably guess what happened next. Alisha knocked herself out putting together those bracelets, working late into the night for a week straight. She sent the bracelets to the company—she had to pay the shipping, of course— and then waited to receive a check. But the check never came. Whenever she called the company to ask about the status of her payment, she was forwarded to voicemail. All her messages went unanswered.

A few weeks later Alisha received a box from the company returning all the bracelets she'd made, along with a letter informing her that her merchandise had been rejected because "unfortunately they did not meet our specifications." Alisha had been scammed out of more than $150, not to mention all the time she'd worked. And all she got in return was a bigger credit card bill and a box full of second-rate bracelets.

The moral of Alisha's story is this: legitimate companies pay YOU to work for THEM, not the other way around. Don't take chances if something seems too good to be true. Don't let desperation blur your vision. There are plenty of genuine money-making opportunties out there. Keep looking.

CHAPTER 3:

KNOW THYSELF

In 2014, commedian Jim Carrey delivered a commencement address at Maharishi University of Management that many call one of the greatest graduation speeches ever given. In this address Carrey explained how he had devoted himself to a "ministry of comedy" as his contribution to the world, and he challenged the graduates to discover and live their own ministries.

"How will you serve the world?" Carrey asked. "What do they need that your talent can provide? That's all you have to figure out."

Of course there was a lot more to Carrey's speech than that, but the underlying theme boiled down to recognizing what you're good at and what you most enjoy doing, and then making a life out of whatever that is.

You may be thinking that it's not particularly important for you to enjoy what you're doing right now because your sole objective is to make some money to pay off a debt, put a kid through college, supplement your retirement income, or save up for a new car or a roof for the house. Or maybe you're totally onboard with the idea of pursuing one of your many passions but you're not sure which one or how to begin. Whatever your mindset, I want to encourage you to go into this pursuit with the expectation that **you will be able to make money doing something you like**. Not only will your earning potential increase when you enjoy what you're doing, but you will also have more fun.

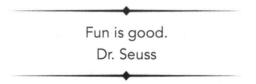

Fun is good.
Dr. Seuss

Unfortunately I've seen a lot of people pick up odd jobs they didn't enjoy because they jumped into the first opportunity that came along. They didn't think things through in advance and as a result made themselves unhappy in exchange for a few bucks a month. For instance, I know a gentleman (I'll call him "Bob") who was forced into retirement at age 58 because the company he worked for was downsizing. Bob had worked for that company his entire adult life. He didn't have any skills that translated to a new position and he wasn't interested in learning something new. So with the sole objective of bringing in a little extra cash each month, he settled on a job he thought would be easy: house cleaning. Every month Bob cleaned four houses and made $500 to supplement his retirement income. Mission accomplished... except that Bob absolutely *hated* cleaning houses. He'd spent the last 35 years working a white collar job in a posh office suite, and suddenly he was scrubbing other people's toilets and mopping other people's floors. The poor guy was miserable, and consequently so were his loved ones. This is not a recipe for a happy retirement.

Bob's troubles could have been avoided if he'd only spent some time up front reflecting on his reasons for finding work and thinking about his preferences, talents and skills. I encourage you to do the same.

Self-Assessment Time

I belong to an incredible professional group, Strategic Coach, which helps entrepreneurs grow their businesses and make their personal lives more balanced and fulfilling. The founder of Strategic Coach, Dan Sullivan, is famous for coming up with what is now known as The Dan Sullivan Question; a one-sentence inquiry that helps people pin down what they'd most like to see happen in their lives. It's one of the quickest ways I know to achieve a sense of clarity for the way forward. Spend a few moments thinking about The Dan Sullivan Question in the context of your current financial situation:

The Dan Sullivan Question

"If we were having this discussion three years from today and you were looking back over those three years, what has to have happened in your life for you to feel happy with your progress?"

Well, what do you think? What must happen over the next three years for you to feel happy with your progress? Perhaps you'd need to have achieved greater financial security for yourself and your family. Or maybe you realized that what you're really looking for is a rewarding way to spend your spare time in retirement. Or maybe you want to give back to your community… put together some money for a trip to Paris… learn a new skill or expand on one you already have… or finally do that thing you're passionate about.

Whatever your answer to The Dan Sullivan Question might be, grab a pen and a piece of paper and write it down right now. If you have more than one answer, rank them in priority order. The writing-it-down part may sound trivial to you, but please don't skip it. Writing stuff down is the key to processing your ideas and turning them into actionable steps. Just ask billionaire investors Warren Buffet and Sir Richard Branson, both of whom swear by jotting down notes as a way of refining their ideas and making them stick. When you make the effort to write your answer to The Dan Sullivan Question on a piece of paper, you are forcing your brain to focus like a laser on that answer. That's because it's impossible to think of anything else when you're engaged in the physical act of writing. Putting pen to paper effectively cements an idea into your conciousness. This is exactly what you want. You want your main objective to be front and center in your mind as you move forward.

Now that you know your overarching goal for the next three years, brainstorm the various ways you could achieve that goal. For instance, if your goal has anything to do with improving your finances, then obviously you'll have to get a job or find a way to provide goods or services to other people in exchange for money. But if your goal is to find a rewarding way to spend your spare time, then you could either get a job, start a business, enroll in a class, volunteer, travel, join a civic group, take up a new hobby... you get the idea. Write down a few of these kinds of "big picture" activities that align with your goal. Don't worry about narrowing it down to any particular job, any particular class, or any particular volunteer opportunity. Think about this from a macro perspective right now.

Let's imagine that your goal is to supplement your retirement income, and you list "get a job" and "provide goods or services to others" as potential ways you could make that happen. Now think about your preferences and the kind of lifestyle you want. Are you a person who likes to be (or must be) close to home most of the day? Are you a night owl or an early bird? Do you enjoy being on-the-go, or do you prefer a slower pace? Are you energized by being part of a group, or do you value your solitude? Do you feel better when your day is structured, or when it's more spontaneous? Write down your preferences.

Now think about your skills and strengths. Jot down the answers to these questions:

- What tasks do I do better than most people? (For example: communicating orally and/or in writing, sales/persuasion, analysis, arts/crafts, physical activities, listening, teaching/explaining, manual tasks, etc.)
- What do my friends and family tell me I do well?
- What are my three greatest character strengths? (For example: honesty, compassion, willpower, gratitude, flexibility, creativity, resilience, patience, work ethic, curiosity, humility, courage, etc.)

Pay attention here, because these are the aspects of yourself that you can leverage as you figure out how you'll meet the objective established via The Dan Sullivan Question (which, to reiterate our example above, was *supplement your retirement income* by *getting a job* or *providing goods or services to others*).

It's time for a little self-disclosure. If I were doing this exercise, I would write that I'm really good at analysis, creative problem solving and persuasion. My family tells me I'm a good listener. My three greatest character strengths are honesty, curiosity and humility and my preference is to work as part of a high-energy group in an engaging environment that provides a lot of variety.

Now I've gained some clarity about myself. Now when I think of all the *specific* ways I could achieve greater financial security through working a job or providing goods or services to others, I can begin to eliminate those opportunities that don't fit my skills, strengths and preferences and instead focus on those that do. For instance, if I come across a part-time job hand-assembling tiny widgets alone in my house, I won't bother applying because I know that doing repetitive manual labor isolated in a quiet room doesn't fit my skills or my preferences.

So often I meet people who haven't asked themselves these questions when they're planning their future. They give little or no thought to the impact a particular job or money-making activity might have on their preferred lifestyle or their natural way of being. Instead of finding a job that fits their personality and the kind of life they want to live, they try to make themselves and their life fit the job. And then they're shocked when they realize how unhappy they are. I am certain that if my friend Bob the House Cleaner had taken the time to answer The Dan Sullivan Question and think about his strengths, skills and preferences before diving headfirst into the house cleaning business, he would never have chosen that path. He could have saved himself and his family a lot of heartache.

Meaning is not something you stumble across,
like the answer to a riddle
or the prize in a treasure hunt.
Meaning is something you build into your life.
John W. Gardner

All this soul searching, reflection and writing stuff down may sound basic to you, but ask yourself this: if it's so basic, why don't more people do it? Why do so many of us jump into things without acquiring the proper perspective first? Perhaps it's because we don't believe we possess the power to create the life we really want. But I'm here to tell you that we **do** possess that power. Sure, luck has something to do with it, but so does *preparation*. As the Roman philosopher Seneca reminds us, "Luck is what happens when preparation meets opportunity."

You are now prepared to view the opportunities we'll discuss in the remainder of this book through the lens of everything you've learned about yourself in this chapter. In other words, you're now better prepared to seize some good luck of your own.

Further Exploration:

- For a free interactive tool that matches your interests with jobs you might enjoy, visit the U.S. Department of Labor's Interest Profiler at www.MyNextMove.org/explore/ip
- For a free "character strengths" assessment, visit www.ViaCharacter.org

Driver Dave

I met "Dave," 67, a few years ago, just as he was starting to put his retirement plans into motion. Dave's retirement income was going to be more than enough to meet his family's needs; in fact, he and his wife were on track to be quite comfortable financially for the rest of their lives. Dave became more and more energized as his retirement date drew near. He couldn't wait to leave his high-voltage executive career behind and start enjoying a life of leisure.

The only problem was that retirement didn't turn out to be nearly as much fun as Dave had anticipated. He was bored out of his mind by the second day.

"I can't stand sitting around like this, Mike," he told me. "I know I don't need the money, but I think I'd feel better if I could be productive again. I'd love to find something fun to do that would bring in an extra couple hundred dollars a month."

I asked Dave about his likes, dislikes, strengths and preferences. One interesting thing we discovered through this questioning was that Dave loves driving. I suggested that he check out some of the car dealerships around town because they sometimes have part-time driving jobs where you can deliver vehicles from one place to another. I also encouraged him to tell all his family and friends that he was looking for a job that involved driving. The more people on the lookout for prospects, the better.

And that's exactly how it shook out. Dave's neighbor heard about a part-time state-funded job driving children with disabilities to and from tutoring sessions, swimming lessons and other recreational activities so their parents didn't have to miss work. She told Dave about it and he applied. After passing the required background check and driving record verifications, he got the job. He picks up a kid in his own car, drives them wherever they need to go, waits an hour while they play or receive tutoring, and then drives them back to Point A. It's around two hours of work at a time, twice a week. In exchange, Dave earns $15 an hour plus mileage and gasoline reimbursement, which amounts to about $240 in extra income each month. It's exactly what he was looking for.

But even more important than the money, the job has been extremely rewarding for Dave from a personal standpoint. It gets him out of the house and gives him something positive to look forward to every week. He loves using one of his favorite skills—driving—to help little kids with disabilities, and by extension, their hardworking families. It is truly one of those rare occasions where everybody wins.

PROVIDING SERVICES FROM HOME

CHAPTER 4:

BEING A REMOTE WORKER—

An Overview and Some Starting Points

A ccording to Global Workplace Analytics, more than 3.7 million people worked from home at least some of the time in 2015—an increase of 103 percent since 2005. While most of these people were full-time employees of a company, many were part-time and/or temporary workers brought in to a fill a role that's suited to working remotely.

There are two things that have led to this explosion of opportunities to work from home. The first is technology like high speed internet and Skype, a software which enables people to speak, message, and hold virtual face-to-face meetings in real time regardless of how many time zones separate them. The second development is the change in attitudes about utilizing remote workers. Companies now understand that not only can they save money by hiring telecommuting workers (as much as $10,000 per worker in savings for office space, absenteeism and turnover, according to Global Workplace Analytics) but the workers are also happier and more productive than on-site employees. In fact, one study found that remote call center workers made 13.5 percent more calls than their office-bound peers, and were half as likely to quit.[4]

Home-based jobs used to be limited to functions like graphic arts and writing, but they've recently been extended to all kinds of positions including customer support, software development, legal services, and even executive-level positions. A terrific example of this is a retired woman I know (I'll call her "Nancy") who has used her extensive accounting and business skills to help companies in need of a temporary chief financial officer (CFO). Nancy is basically a "CFO for rent." She works out of her home office for anywhere from three to 15 companies at a time. These are companies that need an interim CFO to step in for a little while, usually less than six months, until they can hire a replacement for an employee who was let go or one who has retired. Sometimes Nancy works for free because she believes in the business and wants to give back. In other cases she takes an ownership stake in the company in exchange for her work. But most of the time she's paid above-market rates for her expertise. Nancy has been able to leverage her stellar reputation and comprehensive skills in a way that guarantees

---

4   https://hbr.org/2014/01/to-raise-productivity-let-more-employees-work-from-home/ar/1, accessed June 21, 2016.

she's never at a loss for work. And with flexible hours and zero commute, she's never been happier.

You don't have to be an executive-level performer like Nancy to make money working from home. All it takes is a marketable skill (you've probably got more than one of those!) and the knowledge of where to look for work.

How Much Can You Earn?

You can make anywhere from a few dollars a week to six figures a year working from home. Your earnings are totally dependent on your skill set and the amount of time you are able to devote to the task. It doesn't cost a lot to get started working remotely; in fact you've likely got everything you need already. Computer? Check. Internet connection? Check. A burning ambition to make some extra cash this month? Double check.

Who's it For?

Remote work is a good fit for people who are well-organized, confident and disciplined. Let's talk about discipline for a moment. Most people believe that folks who work from home have to be disciplined in order to keep from slacking off, but the remote workers I know tell me the opposite is true: having the self-control to *stop working* is sometimes the greater challenge. Working from home can consume your entire life if you let it, so you must set firm boundaries to make sure you don't overdo it and negatively impact your work/life balance.

You may also have to set boundaries with family members and friends who might think that just because you're home, you're available… for running errands, taking care of kids, going out for an impromptu coffee break. And that's why remote work veterans recommend establishing consistent "office hours," communicating those hours to everyone around you, and then sticking to them as best you can. That way your loved ones (and your clients) will know what to expect from day to day.

Getting Started

The great thing about offering a service from home is that you can give it a try without making a major commitment of time or money. Today's technology makes it relatively easy to find and step into a role, walk around in it for a while and see how you like it. Some of the more popular remote work opportunities are in the following functions:

- Accounting
- Consulting
- Bookkeeping
- Virtual Assistant
- Appointment Setting
- Graphic Design
- Web Development
- Mobile Development
- Writing
- Customer Service
- Sales and Marketing

We'll explore some of these roles in greater detail in subsequent chapters, but for now let me say this: if you already have the skills necessary to do any of these gigs, it's conceivable that you could start earning money today, especially if you're experienced in customer service, user interface design, virtual assistance or web/mobile app development, as these are the fastest growing segments in the work-from-home arena. There are several websites dedicated to linking workers who can perform these types of roles with companies and individuals looking for help. Let's take a look at a few of the more popular ones.

UpWork.com and Guru.com

If you're an aspiring home worker, logging onto Guru or UpWork (formerly known as Elance/Odesk) is like being a little kid in a well-stocked candy store. UpWork calls itself "an online workplace for the world," and that's the perfect way to describe sites like these. You'll see one job listing after another on UpWork, Guru and similar sites... and it's all there just for you, ripe for the picking. Talk about opportunity: workers earned $941 million from 2.8 million job listings on UpWork alone in 2014.[5]

UpWork and Guru provide a platform for job listings posted by clients from all over the world. The sites manage the proposals that candidates submit in response to those job listings, and their system helps clients and their chosen workers come up with fair terms and agreements. They serve as a conduit for making and receiving payments. They mediate any disputes that might arise. And for hourly gigs they even have technology

---

5   http://elance-odesk.com/online-work-report-global, accessed June 22, 2016.

that allows clients to track the true amount of time their hires have worked.

You're usually not considered to be an employee of the people or companies that hire you on sites like UpWork and Guru. Instead, you're an independent contractor. Generally speaking, you're an independent contractor if you supply your own equipment and materials to do a job and if you get to decide when and where you'll work. Conversely, employees receive all the necessary tools and materials from their employer, and they work when and where the employer tells them to. Employees have their taxes withheld by their employer, while independent contractors are responsible for paying their own taxes.

To be able to apply for gigs on these sites, you first have to create an account and pay a small fee, which you'll be charged on a monthly basis. As of right now those monthly fees run anywhere from $10 to $35 dollars depending on the membership level you choose. You'll be asked for your name, address, banking information, and social security number (the social security number is for tax purposes). Then you'll create a profile that details your skills and describes your experience in your chosen job category(s). You'll be given the opportunity to upload a photo of yourself, a resume and references.

Many of these sites also have skills tests you can take to prove your proficiency, with the scores being posted to your profile for all the world to see. For example, writers can take grammar and spelling tests. Bookkeepers can take an exam to prove their competence with QuickBooks. Virtual assistants and customer service reps can take tests to demonstrate their expertise with telephone and email communication. You may have to pay to take some of these tests, but the cost is minimal and it's a terrific way to set yourself apart from the pack.

And now let's talk about "the pack," because it's something you need to be aware of up front. Competition on sites like UpWork and Guru is stiff… extremely stiff. You bid on these jobs, meaning that you have to submit a proposal with the fee you'd charge to do the work and an estimate of the amount of time you think it will take for you to finish it. You'll be competing for the jobs with people from all over the world, many of whom will be able to charge peanuts compared to what the rest of us are used to earning for the same work. But if your skills are solid and if you present yourself professionally *and stick with it,* you really can find and land nice gigs that pay well.

For example, I have a friend whose husband, "Chad," started moonlighting as a graphic designer on one of these sites back in the mid-2000s. His first client was a video poker machine manufacturer who hired him to create on-screen graphics for their machines… graphics like playing cards with various illustrations on the backs, logos, screen designs for all the different themed poker games they were making, and so on. Chad started out earning $200 to $300 from this company every few weeks for the first couple of years. But the company grew to the point where they needed his design services more frequently. They'd become so reliant on Chad that they offered him a retainer of $2,000 a month just to make sure he'd always be available when they needed him.

That arrangement continues to this day, and it has worked out great for both sides. Chad makes enough from this one gig to pay his rent and take his wife out for a nice dinner every month, and most months he doesn't have to do anywhere near $2,000 worth of work. Still, the company thinks it's a great return on their investment. They get guaranteed access to their favorite graphic design professional—on call—for much less than the cost of hiring, training and equipping someone to work in-house. And there's an added bonus for Chad: every time this company pays him they post a glowing review to his online profile, which has made him one of the top-rated graphic artists on the site, worldwide. His business has grown by leaps and bounds as a result. In fact, he was able to quit his day job and now makes a nice living working at home, doing what he loves.

eaHELP.com

Historically, eaHELP was created to fill jobs in one particular profession—that of the virtual executive assistant. But since their founding they have also begun filling social media assistant jobs as well, and other types of work may not be far behind. If you have top-notch administrative support skills, eaHELP is a must-visit site for you.

This award-winning INC 500 company matches clients who are senior-level managers with a dedicated, U.S.-based virtual assistant who handles all the small stuff so the client can focus on the big stuff, like running their business. Virtual assistants do things like managing their client's business and personal calendars, tending to their email and social media accounts, making travel arrangements, event planning, project coordination… whatever the client needs done on a day-to-day basis. Consequently, virtual assistants working through eaHELP should have a bachelor's degree, be extremely well-versed in a variety of skills and technologies, and possess what the company calls "a servant's heart."

eaHELP's virtual assistants work anywhere from five to 20 hours a week during regular business hours. The company doesn't publicize how much it pays its workers but based on the level of expertise they require, it's probably at least market rate or above, which is in the $20 to $45 per hour range for U.S.-based virtual assistants.

FlexJobs.com

More than 1.8 million people have found money-making opportunities via this website, which is billed as "a service that aggregates jobs that offer some type of work flexibility… entry-level to executive; full-time to part-time." For a monthly fee of $14.99 (as of press time), you get access to thousands of current, legitimate, pre-screened, ad- and scam-free job listings for services like consulting, tech and administrative support, sales, customer service, tutoring, accounting, software development, marketing, writing, and much more. And I do mean MUCH MORE. Right now there are over 30,000 job listings from almost 4,500 companies on the site, which is extremely easy to navigate. The site even has categories tailored to specific types of flexible job seekers: freelancers, people with health issues, caretakers, military spouses, retirees, millennials and working parents, to name a few. Not only can you see tons of job listings, but you can also do research about the companies that post them. You can rest assured that the jobs listed here are the real deal; the company says that each one is personally vetted by a FlexJob staffer who may spend as much as 30 minutes making sure they're legit.

All you have to do to get full access to the site is pay your fee, create a profile, choose the kinds of job listings you'd like to see, and then sit back and enjoy the show. Listing after listing after listing of quality money-making opportunities, all consolidated in one place. It's a job seeker's dream. And if you need help you can get it from an actual person via phone or live chat (during regular business hours, of course).

One interesting side note: FlexJobs' entire corporate team works flexible hours from their own homes. It's nice to see a company that actually walks the talk!

LiveOps.com

These days, companies are outsourcing all kinds of functions that used to be done solely in-house. Two of those functions—sales and customer service—can now be accomplished by virtual workers located anywhere in the United States thanks to LiveOps.com. LiveOps is "the premier virtual contact center in the cloud." Companies contract with LiveOps to provide call center services for things like inbound sales and order fulfillment, insurance sales and claims, roadside service, health care, and customer service. LiveOps then contracts with independent agents (people like you) to carry out those services from their homes using LiveOps technology. All you have to have in order to connect to their system is a corded landline phone, a corded headset, and a computer with high speed internet access.

But before you log on, you have to get approved to be one of their independent agents. The approval process is fairly strenuous; not everyone will qualify. You'll fill out an online application and choose the type of call center work you'd like to do (sales, customer service, etc.) You'll complete some questionnaires and assessments to verify that your abilities and skills are a good fit for LiveOps' clients. Once that's done, you'll take part in a voice audition over the phone and submit to checks of your background and credit. If you pass all of that, you'll participate in "onboarding certification" where you'll learn about the companies, products and services you'll be representing, and you'll practice using the LiveOps platform. When you and the LiveOps team think you've got a handle on all this, you'll begin taking calls. *Whew...* you made it!

Pay varies depending on the client and the service you're providing, but it appears to be around $15 per hour. So if you take calls only 15 hours a week, you'll be bringing in an extra $900 a month without ever having to leave your house. I think that's worth all the time and effort it takes to get plugged into the LiveOps system, don't you?

◆

Opportunity Snapshot: Being a Remote Worker
Pros: Inexpensive or free to get started; flexible hours; there is a huge variety of opportunities out there to leverage skills you already have
Cons: Stiff competition; income varies widely; isolation
Best Fit For: People who like to be (or need to be) at home; people who are extremely well-organized, disciplined and who don't give up easily
Tech Savvy Scale: 3—requires use of a computer, digital camera (for uploading your photo to your profiles), Skype, and whatever software is required to do the job

◆

Further Exploration:

- Did you know that Microsoft Office has free templates for making resumes? Visit https://templates.office.com and select "Resumes and Cover Letters" from the list of options.

The Story of Jim, a Very Determined Guy

"Jim" is no stranger to hard work. He's held one or more part-time jobs since the age of 13 when he started working weekends at a neighborhood grocery store. Despite the fact that he had a job and was a busy student athlete, Jim managed to earn straight A's every year. Upon high school graduation he was offered a full scholarship to play basketball at a university on the opposite side of the state. Jim had to give up his old job at the grocery store—a job he'd worked every single weekend of his teens.

As soon as he arrived in his new college town, Jim started looking for opportunities to make some cash. He went to work at a convenience store near campus. It was OK, he made enough to keep himself in spending money. He wished he had a little more though. He didn't like asking his mom for money. She was a hard-working but struggling single mother; it was all she could do to put food on the table for Jim's younger siblings. So when he saw an ad on the Student Union bulletin board that said "run your own business and earn college credit this summer" he jumped at it. It turned out that the opportunity consisted of managing a house painting franchise. The umbrella company went into college towns and recruited bright entrepreneurial students to oversee the franchise from their dorm rooms. Once trained, the student manager was responsible for hiring other students to do the actual painting, and also for marketing the service and securing jobs.

Jim completed his training and hired a dozen of his buddies to do the work. It was an abject failure. He ended up having to fire most of the guys because they wouldn't follow through, and he made very little money. But Jim didn't lose hope. Over the course of the next school year he studied management principles and read a lot of books about customer service. By the time the second summer rolled around he was much better prepared. His sales tripled from the year before, and he went from 12 employees to 50. The third summer saw even more growth. Jim was able to employ more than 100 students. He made more money in three months than many people make in a year.

But perhaps the best outcome of this part-time money-making endeavor was that it proved to Jim what a great manager and motivator he was. With his newfound confidence and that awesome experience under his belt, he took a leap and founded his own consulting firm soon after college graduation. By the time he was 30 he had grown it into a thriving multi-million dollar practice.

The moral of Jim's story is this: no matter how young or old you are or how insignificant an opportunity might seem, you never know where it might lead you. With a little courage and a lot of perseverance, you really can move mountains. You really can change your life.

CHAPTER 5:

FREELANCE WRITING

There's an intriguing new trend in the world today, a trend that you may not have heard much about yet: the "digital nomad" lifestyle. This is where people travel all over the globe visiting interesting places and experiencing other cultures while simultaneously running some sort of freelance business via the internet. These folks are their own bosses. They set their own schedules and they can work from anywhere as long as there's a Wi-Fi connection. Imagine sipping wine at an outdoor café in the shadow of the Eiffel Tower with your laptop on the table beside you, and hitting "send" on an invoice for the blogging assignment you just completed for your client in Singapore. Sounds pretty glamorous, doesn't it, *mon chère*?

But for most of us, trekking around the planet as a digital nomad isn't in the cards for us right now. All we really want to do today is bring in a few extra bucks to make our family's life a little easier. A fulfilling and lucrative way to do that is through freelancing writing.

How Much Can You Earn?

As with most flexible money-making opportunities, you will earn as much from writing as your skills and time commitment will allow—anywhere from a few bucks to hundreds of thousands. To illustrate what I mean, one of my friends started a food blog a few years ago. She spends less than 12 hours a week on it, but she makes several hundred dollars a month from advertising because she has developed a good following. She also uses her blog to get discounts by going to vendors and saying that she will blog about them if they give her a price break on their product or service. She figures she saves a couple hundred dollars a month that way. Nice! But check this out: she told me that she has friends whose blogs have become so popular that they were able to quit their day jobs. They are now bringing in well over six figures a year in advertising revenue… and that's in addition to the endorsements they receive from sponsoring companies.

Who's it For?

You don't have to be the next Mark Twain, but you do have to have strong grammar, spelling and storytelling skills. People in lots of different professions have the potential to make money from writing. For instance, teachers usually make great freelance writers because they know the grammar rules and they also know how to explain complex topics in a simple way. People in the legal and medical fields can parlay their expertise into a lucrative freelance writing specialty. I know of a police officer who moonlights as a freelance writer. She honed her skills composing detailed crime reports, and now she writes magazine articles on the topics of personal safety and home security. And I heard of a retired engineer who built a part-time business doing technical writing for manufacturers. He creates the package inserts that explain to consumers how to use and/ or assemble a product. It's complicated work, but he loves it.

Generally speaking, freelance writers have to be dedicated to meeting (or preferably, *beating*) deadlines. Chronically-late procrastinators need not apply. And to meet their clients' stringent expectations, they also have to be great listeners who are detail-oriented. "T"-crossing and "I"-dotting must be an obsession.

Getting Started

There are many different ways to earn money as a freelance writer, including but not limited to the following roles:

- Blogging
- Editing and proofreading other peoples' work
- Writing articles for print magazines and e-zines
- Freelance journalism
- Ghostwriting
- Document translation
- Managing social media for businesses and individuals

- Writing books and e-books (fiction and nonfiction for children, middle-readers, young adults and adults)
- Technical writing
- Creating curriculum and/or courses
- Writing newsletters for schools, churches, civic groups, businesses
- Creating content for websites
- Grant writing

To get a client to hire you for gigs like these, you'll first have to prove to them that you know what you're doing. You accomplish that by showing examples of your work, sometimes referred to as "clips." Building a portfolio of clips is easy if you've already done some writing for your day job (i.e. the engineer I told you about; a teacher who has developed curriculum for years; a retired journalist). But if you want to get hired to do a type of writing you haven't done before, you'll have to get creative.

For example, small community newspapers are usually woefully understaffed and stretched to the limit. So contact your local paper and offer to write about community activities like the annual garden club expo, an upcoming arts festival, or youth sporting events. I know one freelance writer who did this and it worked out great for her. She is into green living, so she offered to write a weekly column for her town's paper about reducing, reusing, recycling and other eco tips. They agreed and paid her $75 per column. She then branched out into writing about environmentally-friendly business practices, which earned her a spot in the paper's monthly business insert for an additional

$100 in earnings. She gets a huge kick out of this gig. Not only is she making money, but she's also educating the people in her community on a topic she's passionate about. She has built an outstanding portfolio of clips and is now using them to market her writing skills to well-known green living magazines, which pay up to $1,500 per article. She accomplishes all of this from the comfort of her own home using only email and Microsoft Word.

Another way to build your stash of clips is to reach out to a non-profit whose work you admire and ask if you can write something for them at no cost in exchange for a testimonial. They will likely jump at the opportunity. Take good care of yourself here: make sure the project has a clear starting and ending point, and keep it small (in other words, you probably shouldn't agree to create a complicated 100-page report for free!).

Once you've compiled some stellar clips, you can visit some of the popular sites that cater to freelance writers. Let's take a look at a few of them.

Listverse.com and TopTenz.com

It turns out that David Letterman isn't the only Top Ten list maker in the world. Lots of folks make lists—and get paid to do so—through websites like Listverse and TopTenz. These sites publish several top ten lists every day, so they need to buy lots of interesting content. Right now Listverse pays $100 per list and TopTenz pays $50.

To get a list published on Listverse and TopTenz, you'll write the piece and email it to the editors. They'll look it over and contact you with their decision. Both sites make a point of saying that they only want lists that are provocative and counterintuitive. If you can make it funny and/or bizarre, all the better. Some lists recently published on Listverse and TopTenz include "10 Creepy Stories from Funeral Homes and Crematoriums," "10 Passengers Forced to Become Pilots Midair," "10 Little-Known Facts about the Anglo-Saxons," and "10 Simple Steps to Earn $100 Writing for Listverse" (you might want to Google that one ASAP!)

These sites have a very specific style, so visit each one and study the kind of stuff they publish before sitting down and making your list.

AListApart.com and UXBooth.com

A List Apart seeks thought-provoking, in-depth articles related to the internet industry on subjects like web development and design, software, coding, user experience, web content writing, project management, e-commerce development, and more. The website says its editors want to hear from you "if you've got an idea that will challenge our readers and move our industry forward." They publish feature stories of 1,500 to 2,500 words; articles of 600 to 1,500 words; and mini-articles of 500 to 600 words. Right now the pay runs from $50 to $200 per piece. You'll find a very helpful guide to writing for A List Apart at http://alistapart.com/about/style-guide.

There's something similar going on over at UXBooth, which is an informative site for people working in the internet arena as user experience or interaction designers. If you have technical tips or tricks for making the World Wide Web more user-friendly, this is the place for you. UXBooth editors are looking for research-based freelance articles in the 1,200 to 1,800 word range, for a current payout of $100.

InternationalLiving.com and MatadorNetwork.com

If you live outside the United States for all or part of the year, the editors at *International Living* and their readers are eagerly awaiting your reports. *International Living* has been around since the 1980s and they operate with one goal in mind: giving people all the information they need to retire overseas successfully.

This publication is looking for quick firsthand stories from expats who can write informative, entertaining segments they call "Daily Postcards." Coming in at only 500 to 600 words, these brief articles are focused on "delightful opportunities for fun... pleasure... financial security and profits... romantic discoveries... [and] adventure" abroad. Each published submission earns the writer $75. The editors make a point of saying that you don't have to be a professional writer to submit a Daily Postcard. All you have to do is tell them something good; something positive you'd like to share with the folks back home about your experience as a retired person living overseas. It could be about art. Culture. Real estate. Inexpensive health care options. An exotic destination. In other words, if it delights you and your expatriate friends, you can share it with *International Living* and get paid to do so.

But you don't have to actually live overseas to earn money sharing stories about the fabulous places you've been. *Matador Network* is always looking for contributors to submit articles, videos and photographs that "speak to the adventures, cultures, and identities of people around the world." Payment starts at $40 for articles of no more than 1,500 words; the pay rate for photos and videos is negotiable.

iWriter.com and TextBroker.com

These sites offer lots of opportunities to write articles, blog posts, e-books and more. At iWriter you'll open an account (it's free) and immediately receive access to postings from "requesters" looking for articles with various projected word counts on a variety of subjects. You click on the posting, read the instructions for what the requester is looking for, and then you start writing. Once you finish the article and upload it to the site, the requester has 72 hours to approve or reject it. Writing for iWriter is a crapshoot because if the requester rejects your article, you don't get paid. But if they accept it, you do. The amount you make per article is established by your status on the iWriter platform. For example, when you first open your account you're considered to be a "Standard" writer and your pay is low (currently $2.43 for 500 words). As you start racking up successful projects and earning positive ratings from the article requesters, you will move up to "Elite" status and ultimately, "Premium," where you'll earn more per article.

TextBroker is similar to iWrite in the sense that businesses and individuals "order" articles on all kinds of topics, with work-at-home writers scrambling to be the one to fill the order and earn the pay check. It's free to get started, and you'll have immediate access to thousands of opportunities to write for money. When you upload your articles to the site, TextBroker editors will rate them and give you feedback on how to improve them. The pay is low to start, but according to the site, "the better your content, the more you can earn." For example, a writer who has achieved a 5-star rating will make $75 for a 1,500 word article.

FundsForWriters.com

This helpful site was created by a veteran freelance writer *for* freelance writers, and it's a treasure trove of valuable "tips and tools for serious writers to advance their careers." Through its newsletters and the website itself, Funds for Writers (FFW) gives you the latest scoop on paying markets for freelance writing as well as competitions, grants, literary agents, publishers and employment for writers. There are two newsletters: the first is a free weekly snapshot of paying opportunities for writers; the second, Total Funds for Writers, costs $18.75 per year and gives subscribers five times more information than the freebie.

FFW also buys short freelance articles on the business of writing. The pay for those is currently $50.

Before you attempt to write an article meant for a particular website, spend some time reading the site first. Pay attention to the overarching tone of the articles, because you'll want to tailor your approach to what's already been successfully published there. Are the articles they publish light-hearted, or serious? Relaxed or formal? Research-based, or anecdotal? Also make sure that the topic of the article you're planning hasn't already been covered there recently. If it has, then be prepared to explain how your approach to the subject is different.

ThePennyHoarder.com

With more than ten million readers every month, The Penny Hoarder (TPH) is the most popular personal finance blog in the world. TPH is always seeking interesting, practical stories about earning, saving and investing money in the categories "Money Hacks," "Work from Home," "Budgeting," "Coupons" and "Freebies." Some of their most popular articles are: *My Family Lives Off One Income After I Had to Leave My Job. Here's How We Budget on a $25,000 Salary; 12 College Majors That Pretty Much Guarantee You'll Land a Better Job; and 10 Ridiculous Ways You're Throwing Away Thousands of Dollars Each Year.* If you have personal experience with anything like this, writing for TPH could be just the ticket for bringing in a little extra cash this month. Their editors are seeking "bloggy, friendly" articles and lists of between 700 and 900 words with real world examples backed up by step-by-step instructions for how to implement your tip(s). Pay is $75, currently. For details, visit www.thepennyhoarder.com/contributor-guidelines/.

WordPress.org, Tumblr.com, Blogger.com, etc.

Another way to make money with your writing is through blogging. A blog is simply a frequently updated website with a conversational style of writing on a particular topic. Common topics for blogs are cooking, travel, sports, technology, shopping, homemaking, green living, pets, specific hobbies, parenting… almost anything goes. There are even blogs about blogging! In addition to the written content, blogs often contain photographs and videos, and they usually have space at the bottom of each post for readers to comment and interact with the blogger and each other.

You start a blog by going to one of the blog publishing websites like WordPress, Tumblr, or Blogger and simply opening an account. They'll walk you through the entire process, which includes providing templates you can use to design your blog any way you like. It's easy to do and in most cases, it's free.

It takes time and effort to earn money from a blog, but the payoff can absolutely make it worthwhile. As I stated earlier, I have a friend who earns and also saves several hundred dollars a month from her part-time blogging project, and she knows others pulling in six figures from their blogs. First and foremost, to have that kind of success you have to choose an interesting subject for your blog, preferably something you're really passionate and knowledgeable about. You have to keep the blog current by updating it often with appealing and useful content. You have to build an audience for your content (the bigger and more engaged the audience, the better). And you have to "monetize" the site somehow, meaning you have to implement a way to generate revenue through the blog.

There are several methods for monetizing a blog. The first is through **advertising** in the form of display ads, banners, etc. Every time someone clicks on an ad on your blog, you make money. It's only a few cents per click but it can really add up (this is why you want the biggest audience possible.) You can either negotiate ad deals directly with the advertiser or go through a middleman, i.e. an ad network like Google's AdSense.

Another way to make money from your blog is to engage in **affiliate marketing**. This is an arrangement between you and an individual or company in which you agree to install a hyperlink to their product or service in your blog's content. When a reader clicks on the link, you get paid for making the referral. Again, it's only pennies per click.

The next money-making opportunity via a blog consists of **selling products and/or services** through your site. These could be digital products like e-books, courses, music, photos and videos (you have to own the copyright to those, of course!); or actual products like handcrafted items, printed books, or anything else that's tangible and somehow related to the subject of your blog. You could also sell services like coaching, tutoring, web development, writing…any service that can be provided remotely can be promoted and sold through your blog.

Opportunity Snapshot: Freelance Writing
Pros: Inexpensive or free to get started; flexible hours; lots of opportunities
Cons: Extremely stiff competition; income varies widely and is not guaranteed; isolation
Best Fit For: People who are good listeners, detail-oriented, punctual; those who are great storytellers and who possess good grammar and spelling skills
Tech Savvy Scale: 2—requires use of a computer and ability to navigate relatively simple websites

---

Further Exploration:

- Professional writers use "style guides" to help them understand and adhere to grammar, spelling, punctuation, common word usage and other rules specific to the various types of publications for which they write. For example, journalists and news media folks consult the most current version of the *Associate Press (AP) Stylebook* while most other writers and publishers refer to *The Chicago Manual of Style.* You can get both of these books at any bookstore or by visiting www.apstylebook.com and www.chicagomanualofstyle.org.

- There is a wealth of information out there about how to start blogging for money. Two good sources are www.amylynnandrews.com and www.problogger.net/make-money-blogging/.

Meet Tanya... The Shotgun Approach to Earning Money

When "Tanya," 60, was fired from her long-time position as regional director of a service franchise following a conflict with a junior colleague, she was devastated. She had never been fired from a job in her life. Tanya had always assumed she would retire from that job and go on to live the rest of her years as a doting grandma, maybe volunteering at the library and serving on the museum board. And now here she was, a divorced woman with five grown sons, three daughters-in-law, two precious grandbabies, a mortgage... and no job. It took Tanya a couple of weeks before she could finally admit to her friends and family that she'd been sacked. They were all as stunned as she was.

But in spite of her anxiety and embarrassment, Tanya soon decided that there was only person on earth who could fix this problem, and it was her. She swallowed her pride and started making phone calls and sending emails, reaching out to everyone she'd ever worked with (a lot of people from coast to coast!) and asking to be considered for any remote gigs they might have. Several people offered her ongoing virtual assistant work like bookkeeping, newsletter writing and transcription. She also opened an Etsy shop with one of her crafty sons. He sold his lovely hand-carved walking sticks while Tanya, a skilled seamstress, offered the pretty little bibs and organic cloth diaper covers she'd become so adept at making for her grandbabies. Thanks to some promotion on social media (which Tanya learned to do on the fly), the shop turned out to be a success.

By networking and cobbling together income here and there—and by maintaining a positive, can-do attitude about her situation—Tanya was able to make enough money to stay afloat for the five months it took to secure another full-time job in her field. As she learned first-hand, the solution to a problem doesn't always have to be a grand one. Every little bit really does help.

CHAPTER 6:

A FEW MORE WORK-FROM-HOME OPPORTUNITIES

I want to tell you about several additional opportunities to make money working from home. These are interesting activities that don't fit neatly anywhere else in this section, so I've given them a chapter all their own. You might find a couple of these pursuits to be unusual. None of them will make you a member of the Rockefeller family overnight, but you really can earn money by doing them, and you'll probably have some fun too.

"Working" through Swagbucks.com

Swagbucks bills itself as "the fun rewards program that gives you gift cards and cash for the everyday things you do online." Those "everyday things" include shopping at your favorite retailers like Amazon, Wal-Mart, Target and Best Buy; searching the internet; watching videos; taking surveys; etc. As of right now, the site has given out over $135 million in cash and gift cards to its members for doing those simple activities— activities they were already happy to do even when they weren't getting paid.

Here's how to get in on the action: go to the Swagbucks website and sign up to become a member. It's easy (all you have to do is enter your email address and create a password) and it's free. You're then taken to a page that shows you a bunch of things you can do to begin earning Swag Buck points, which are also known as "SB." For example, I just logged on to the site and earned 50 SB for signing up for the newsletter at Zulily. com. I earned another 4 SB for taking a one minute survey about my preferences regarding cola drinks. And I'm going to earn 500 SB when I go to Target this weekend and buy two boxes of a particular brand of garbage bag (500 SB equals $5). The website keeps track of how much SB you've earned and displays it in the upper right hand corner of the screen, so it's easy to track your progress. Once you've accumulated a certain amount of SB points, you'll be able to redeem them in exchange for gift cards to popular retailers, or for cash back via PayPal.

Again, nobody's getting rich through Swagbucks, but every little bit helps. Why not give it a try the next time you've got a few minutes to kill?

Taking Online Surveys

If you're like the majority of people, you enjoy giving your opinion. Whether it's about the quality of the new restaurant down the street, the candidates in an upcoming election, your city's sports teams or the latest fashion, most of us love to tell others what we think. And now, thanks to several survey websites, you can get paid to share your views.

Three of the most popular of these sites—GlobalTestMarket. com, EPollSurveys.com, and SurveyClub.com—reward their members for giving their opinions on all kinds of products and services.

Not all survey-taking opportunities are created equal; in fact, there are a lot of scams around this type of work. As always, use caution when signing up for any work-at-home gig. Check out the opportunity carefully (refer back to Chapter 2 for tips on avoiding scams) and guard your personal information like a hawk until you are certain the entity is legit.

For now, let's focus on Global Test Market. This site is run by a company that does market research for over 1,400 businesses worldwide. The topics for the surveys include movies, restaurants, cars and scads of consumer products. You are only allowed to take a particular survey if you fit the demographic the brands are trying to reach, as evidenced by the profile information you filled out upon becoming a member of the site. For example, a baby food company will only want to hear from women who are mothers of small children; a business suit manufacturer will be targeting professional men between the ages of 25 and 65; a multi-vitamin for seniors will only want to survey people over a certain age, and so on.

Some of the surveys take a couple of minutes to finish while others can take half an hour or more. Like at Swag Bucks, every activity you complete earns you points that can be redeemed for cash and gift cards. Today the average pay per survey on Global Test Market is $5.[6] I recognize that $5 is not much, but it can add up if you stick with it. Think about it: if you could qualify for and complete one survey every day for 30 days, you'd have $150 in your pocket at the end of the month. If you kept this up for a year, you'd have an extra $1,800. I imagine you could find a very good use for $1,800, right?

The cool thing about taking online surveys is that unlike most other make-money-at-home opportunities, you don't need to have any particular skill to do it, nor do you have to have a product to sell or a service to provide. All it requires is that you sit at your computer, answer a few questions about your preferences, and watch the points build up. Sweet!

UserTesting.com

See if you can relate to this... you visit a website to buy a product (say, a bouquet of flowers for your mom who lives halfway across the country). You spend several minutes choosing the perfect flowers. You spend another several

---

6   https://www.globaltestmarket.com/make_money_online.php, accessed June 30, 2016.

minutes painstakingly entering all of your shipping and billing information, as well as creating a "Happy Birthday Mom! Love, Me XO" greeting card to be included in the delivery. You double-check all your info and when you're satisfied that it's correct, you hit "Complete My Order." But for some reason the order doesn't go through; you get taken back to the home page instead. You shrug it off and do the whole thing over again, only to end up right back where you started once again. The flower shop's website has an annoying bug, you just wasted half an hour, and your mom's still not getting her bouquet.

This is where UserTesting.com comes in. User Testing links its members (known as testers) with website owners who want their site analyzed for ease of use and the presence of any bugs. The User Testing technology allows you, the tester, to go to a website and try to navigate it to accomplish a short list of prescribed tasks while simultaneously recording your audio comments the entire time. The website owner gets the results of each test, which gives them invaluable feedback about the real-world experience a new user had while navigating their site. The tester earns $10 per test. Each test takes an average of ten to 20 minutes to complete, so it's the equivalent of earning $30 to $60 per hour.

In my view, User Testing is one of the more interesting ways to work from home. Not only are you having fun exploring new websites, but you're also earning money AND helping make the internet more user-friendly. Everybody wins.

Izea.com

It's tough to promote a brand online these days. Competition is stiff, and consumers don't respond to banner ads and other internet marketing ploys like they used to. In fact, it's been proven that internet users are increasingly ignoring these types of ads in a phenomenon called "banner blindness." Whether banner blindness is a function of our subconscious minds or a conscious decision, the truth is we just don't react to online ads that much anymore. Consequently, advertisers are having to get creative in order to get their brands in front of the right consumers.

Enter Izea, which "connects influential content Creators with the world's biggest brands." In other words, Izea links brand marketers with people who have a large following online—popular bloggers, celebrities, Twitter users, YouTubers, Facebook-ers, Instagram-ers, etc.—so they can form a mutually-beneficial partnership. The brand essentially underwrites content on these high-profile sites, paying the creator of the content (that would be you) to promote their brand to your existing audience of followers. This gets the brand seen by large numbers of people and pays sponsorship money to the content creator (again, that would be you).

To get in on the "sponsored content" game, you first have to be a blogger with a healthy following. You then create an Izea account and start getting connected to companies that are trying to reach your type of audience. For example, if you run a popular blog about barbeque and the Char-Broil grill company is looking for sponsored content, the Izea platform would hook you two up, in the virtual sense. Consider it like Match.com for content creators and related brands who are looking for love.

There is big money in sponsored content if you've got a large enough audience. Keep this in mind as you build your online presence. Even if you're not quite there today, it's a good goal to have.

Doing Transcription

If you like to type and you're good at it—and by that I mean *REALLY* good at it—you can make decent money working part-time from home as a transcriptionist. There are several platforms for finding transcription work online, but two of the better known are SpeakWrite.com and FastChart.com. Speak Write is for general transcription as well as transcription for the legal community, law enforcement and protective services while Fast Chart is for medical transcription only. It works like this: somewhere in the world right now, a lawyer who subscribes to Speak Write is recording notes about her latest court case using the Speak Write app on her smartphone (or any digital recording device). She sends the audio file to Speak Write, which assigns one of its remote typists to listen to the recording and transcribe it. When the transcription is complete, the typist receives a portion of the money the lawyer paid to Speak Write for their services. According to Speak Write, the average typist earns $300 a month while top earners are raking in over $3,000 monthly.

These sites require that you be able to type a minimum speed with a certain level of accuracy. You will be tested on that before being approved. You also have to show that you've got experience as a legal, medical or general transcriptionist in an office environment, and you must have earphones and a newer version of Microsoft Word, Adobe Reader, Windows and internet browser. And because of the sensitive information you'll have access to in this role, you also have to pass a series of background checks which are paid for by the company. To find out more about partnering with Speak Write or Fast Chart, visit http://speakwrite.com/transcription-jobs/ and http://www.fastchart.com/about/careers/.

LeapForceAtHome.com

If you enjoy surfing the internet, this is the gig for you. As a Leapforce independent agent, you will "conduct in depth internet-based research and provide information evaluation for leading companies from around the globe." In other words, your task will be to do search engine evaluation for Leapforce's clients. The job consists of checking internet search results to make sure they are relevant to what was typed into the search bar. For example, if I google "Baltimore Ravens," I would expect to see the official National Football League's Baltimore Ravens website near the top of the search results. But if instead I see that an obscure blog about Edgar Allan Poe's "The Raven," has come in higher in the search ranking than the Baltimore Raven's site, I would know that something is amiss. Search engine evaluators are the folks paid to catch these types of anomalies and report them to whichever client has hired them to conduct the check.

In addition to a computer, high speed internet and the latest Google Chrome browser, you'll also need a strong knowledge of internet research to do this kind of work. You must have sharp analytical skills and the ability to communicate effectively in writing. And if you have command of any languages in addition to English, Leapforce is especially eager to partner with you.

Your skills and proficiency in all aspects of the work will be tested before you're approved. People who have taken the Leapforce exams report that they are fairly difficult. Even though Leapforce provides extensive study materials, not everyone will pass the tests. There is also training involved; training for which you will not be compensated. But if you can get through it and be approved as an agent, you can work from home earning in the neighborhood of $13 per hour.

Upgrade Your Retirement Income

Let's imagine for a moment that a recent retiree, "Lillian," decides to use the information in this chapter to generate some extra cash working from home to supplement her social security income. Every morning Lillian sits down at her kitchen table with a cup of coffee, logs on to GlobalTestMarket.com and takes a survey. For an hour on Monday, Wednesday and Friday afternoons she does some transcription for FastChart.com, after which she updates her blog about achieving fulfillment in retirement. On Tuesday and Thursday mornings she spends three hours doing user testing for UserTesting.com. Whenever she has a few minutes to kill, she logs onto Swagbucks and earns some quick SBs.

Lillian spends 12 to 15 hours each week on her various work-from-home activities, which serves several important purposes. It keeps her engaged in the world around her. It's fun, challenging and interesting. It gives her something gratifying to look forward to every day. It impresses her grandkids, who think it's pretty cool that their Grandma Lilly is so plugged in to today's technology. And finally, it's lucrative. Lillian earns from $1,200 to as much as $2,000 a month this way, which supplements her social security income very nicely.

If Lillian can do it, so can you!

---◆---

Opportunity Snapshot:
Miscellaneous Work-at-Home Gigs
Pros: Inexpensive or free to get started; very flexible hours; interesting opportunities; some require no special skills
Cons: Income varies widely and is not guaranteed; isolation
Best Fit For: People who need to or want to work from home; those who enjoy working on the computer
Tech Savvy Scale: 2 to 4—requires use of a computer and ability to navigate websites; other opportunities require use of special software or equipment.

---◆---

Further Exploration:

- Similar to Swag Bucks is www.InboxDollars.com, where you get rewarded for taking surveys, playing games, shopping and redeeming coupons. As I write this, you can earn $5 just for signing up.

Meet Janet... On the Road Again

At the end of her 30-year career as a trooper patrolling the highways of her home state, "Janet" thought she was ready for a rest. But she quickly learned that a retirement spent sitting around the house doing nothing was not her idea of a good time. At 58 she still had a lot of energy and a lot of life ahead of her. She needed to come up with something that challenged her and made her look forward to getting out of bed in the morning. And if she could make a little money to supplement her pension and investment income, all the better. Her son would be entering his junior year of college soon, and another round of tuition payments was about to be due.

Janet started brainstorming about what she might do. She settled on finding a way to leverage the extensive experience and knowledge she'd accumulated during her long career in law enforcement. Teaching came to mind... she'd taught occasional classes at the law enforcement academy in the past and had enjoyed it. But she didn't want to be confined to a strict schedule like that now. She wanted something with flexible hours, and she also wanted to travel. She kept on thinking...

One evening she was watching the news and saw a story about a trucking company that had just been slapped with hefty fines for violating various transportation safety regulations. The reporter interviewed the trucking company's CEO and he remarked on how hard it was to keep up with all the regulations nowadays. *"Huh,"* Janet thought. *"He should have called me. I know ALL the regulations!"*

And then a wild idea popped into Janet's head: what if she could become a consultant to transportation companies around the country to inform them on and help them comply with industry regulations? She'd get to use her knowledge and her teaching skills to make the world a safer place. She'd get to travel. And she'd make enough money that she wouldn't have to dip into her savings account to pay her son's tuition.

Janet quickly put together an updated resume listing her areas of expertise and started reaching out to her connections. She'd made a lot of them during her law enforcement career… and not all of them were negative! Janet was amazed at how eager everyone was to help her expand her network and launch her fledgling business.

Within six months of having her epiphany about becoming a consultant, Janet was meeting with her first client. Now she travels from coast to coast advising transportation companies on regulatory compliance issues. The companies love having her on their team. Even though they're paying her quite well, she's still saving them tons of money because they're not being fined anymore. Janet is thrilled with the challenge and flexibility of her new gig, and she's also thrilled that she earns more than enough to pay her son's college tuition.

PROVIDING SERVICES IN YOUR COMMUNITY

CHAPTER 7:

DRIVING FOR DOLLARS

I n 2009, a technological and social phenomenon began sweeping across America when a new online transportation network, Uber, was launched. Uber's mission was to simplify the way people get from place to place within their city, and they have certainly achieved their goal. Now rather than driving or taking a bus, train or taxi, people can use their smart phones to hail a quick low-cost ride from an Uber driver or one of the other transportation networks, including Lyft, which have cropped up across the country over the past several years. We're going to focus on Uber in this chapter because it's the most popular and has the greatest reach. The good news is that all of the transportation networks function in pretty much the same way.

Here's how it works: wannabe riders download a free app to their smart phone. They use the app to register as an Uber customer, and they enter their credit or debit card information to be kept on file. From then on, whenever they need a ride, they open the app and tap the "Get a Ride" button, which connects them to the smart phone of the nearest approved Uber driver—an independent contractor operating his or her own personal vehicle. The driver accepts the ride request and begins making his/her way to the rider's location. Up pops a picture of the driver and a description of the vehicle on the rider's phone. The rider can even track the vehicle as it makes its way to their location. Upon arrival the rider tells the driver where they want to go, and the driver takes them there. The app charges the rider's credit card automatically for the cost of the fare when the trip is complete. The transaction is totally electronic; no cash changes hands unless the rider wants to tip the driver. Uber keeps a percentage of the fare (around 20 percent) and gives the rest to the driver.

At the end of each trip the Uber app prompts both the rider and the driver to rate one another on a scale of one to five stars. This serves as a reference check of sorts, because if your ratings fall too low as either a driver or a rider, you lose access to the system.

As I write this, Uber operates in over 450 cities worldwide and has more than 8 million customers. To meet the needs of that many riders, Uber needs drivers... lots and lots and lots of drivers. It's relatively easy to supplement your income by becoming an Uber driver. You can work as little or as much as you want. You set your own hours, and you can focus on serving a particular neighborhood or an entire city… it's all up to you. You're in the driver's seat, Boss.

How Much Can You Earn?

According to Uber.com, drivers using their technology earn an average of $19.04 per hour. How much you earn depends on how often you drive. But remember, this is gross pay, not net. As an independent contractor you have to set aside a portion of your earnings to pay your taxes, and you also have to pay for your own gas, car insurance and vehicle maintenance. Uber deposits your earnings directly into your bank account on a weekly basis.

Who's It For?

You must be at least 21-years old to become an Uber driver. You have to have a good driving record, pass a background check and carry current liability insurance on your vehicle. Your car must be a 4-door, model year 2000 or newer (minimum 2005 model year in some cities). The vehicle has to be clean, odor-free and in excellent condition with no dents or dings. It has to have good tires and functioning windshield wipers, headlights, blinkers, horn and seat belts; in short, everything has to work properly. No clunkers allowed. And obviously you have to live in or near a city where Uber operates, and you have to have a smart phone.

NEWS FLASH!

Don't currently have a vehicle that meets Uber's or Lyft's requirements? No problem! Both transportation networks have partnered with car leasing and rental companies including Toyota, Volkswagen, GM and Enterprise to give their drivers reduced rates on vehicle leases and weekly rentals. Lease and rental payments are made directly from the driver's earnings.

———————◆———————

The best Uber drivers are calm and punctual. They know their way around town. They like variety, a fast pace, and meeting new people. They have a service-oriented personality, meaning they are driven (pardon the pun) to make people happy. They are skilled at gauging other people's moods, too. For example, some riders like to chat during the trip while others want peace and quiet. The highest-rated drivers are quick to detect these sorts of preferences and always respect them. And most of all, successful Uber drivers are people who really enjoy driving. They know the traffic laws and they follow them to a T.

I have a friend (I'll call him "Alex") who is a great example of the perfect Uber driver. Alex was an early adopter of Uber. He possessed all the desirable qualities to be a driver and he also had a suitable car, but he took a bit of a detour before actually climbing behind the wheel.

Alex began using Uber's services as a rider when the company was first trying to get off the ground, and he loved it. Uber offers rewards for referring friends to use their services as either a driver or a rider, meaning that whenever you refer someone and they sign up and use the service, both you and your friend received $5 in Uber credit. Back when Uber started they were offering $10 credit. As a huge fan of Uber, Alex was recommending friends left and right. He started to rack up a hefty pile of credit, which caught the attention of the company. They approached Alex and told him that he was in the top ten percent of all referrals so they were going to give him and his friends double the reward everyone else received, a $20 deal for each. Alex was smart. He listed this awesome Uber credit offer on the coupon website Retailmenot.com. While everyone else on the site was offering the normal $10 Uber promotion, Alex was the only one with the $20 deal. He got over 200 replies the first weekend alone and accumulated over $4,000 in Uber credit. He went three years without ever having to pay an Uber fare.

Back then Alex worked for a federal contractor. The government was going through sequestration at the time and had cut off a lot of contract work. So although Alex was still getting paid by his employer, he didn't have much to do. He was starting to get bored; plus he was saving up for an engagement ring and wanted to make some extra cash for that. He had talked to many Uber drivers over the years and learned that you could make decent money driving in your spare time, so he decided to give it a try. His plan was to drive when he had nothing to do at work and also on one weekend night each week. Friday and Saturday nights are peak service times for Uber. Their drivers get a higher rate whenever demand is heavy (this is called "surge pricing"). Alex's rational was that not only would he make a couple hundred dollars a night, he would also save money by not going out for dinner and drinks with his friends. Alex made around $9,000 as an Uber driver that year and figures he saved at least another $3,000 by not going out so often. Consequently, Alex's part-time stint as an Uber driver covered much of the cost of his fiancé's engagement ring.

Getting Started

Signing up to be an Uber driver is surprisingly quick, free and easy. You can get approved and start driving in as little as 48 hours. Here's how it works.

Visit Uber.com and click on "Become a Driver." You'll be prompted to create an account with your name, phone number, email address and a description of your car. You're then asked for your social security number, which Uber needs in order to run a background check on you. No worries; the background check is confidential and doesn't affect your credit rating. You can request to receive a free copy of the results of the background check if you're interested in seeing it.

Next you'll be required to upload photographs of your driver's license, car insurance card and vehicle registration. Uber will confirm that all of these driving documents are in good standing before approving you to hit the road. Note that Uber provides up to $1 million in liability coverage for you from the time you accept each ride request until the time that ride is complete. However, you're still required to carry sufficient auto insurance to cover you before and after that.

After your documents are uploaded, you'll be prompted to download the Uber app to your smart phone. Once Uber notifies you that you've been approved, you'll go into the app to set up your tax and banking account information so you can get paid. Whenever you're ready to begin driving—whether it's for an hour or for the entire day—you simply sign in to the Uber app with your user name and password and start receiving trip requests.

Now you're in business!

Opportunity Snapshot: Driving for Dollars

Pros: Free to get started; flexible hours; cashless transactions; earn credit for making referrals; quick payment

Cons: Strict requirements (late model car, clean driving record, no criminal history); driver pays for gas and vehicle maintenance

Best fit for: People who want or need flexible hours; those who enjoy meeting new people and working with the public

Tech Savvy Scale: 2—requires use of a smart phone and app

Further Exploration:

- To find out if Uber operates in your locale, visit www.uber.com/cities; to check into Lyft, visit www.lyft.com/cities.

CHAPTER 8:

CAREGIVING

To be happy and to achieve our full potential as individuals and as members of society, we human beings require care. That's why I believe that if you have a caring nature, the world is your oyster. *We need you.* So if you get joy from taking care of little children, helping seniors or people with disabilities, tending to animals, gardens or other peoples' homes... there are folks looking for your help right now, and they're willing to pay a pretty penny for your services.

The trick is in figuring out how to connect with those people in need in your community. Luckily, making those connections is not all that tricky anymore thanks to today's technology.

How Much Can You Earn?

Your earnings as a caregiver will depend on the type of care you're providing, the going rate in your particular market, and how often you're willing or able to work. Here are the median hourly pay rates for some common caregiving jobs in the United States right now, according to PayScale.com:[7]

- Child care provider: $10
- Dog sitter: $11
- Dog walker: $12
- House cleaner: $11
- Gardener: $13
- Elder care (non-nurse): $10
- Elder care (LPN): $19
- Respite care: $10

Again, pay rates will vary depending on your location and your experience level. Remember: in most cases you have the freedom to experiment by setting your own rates and seeing how it works out. Nothing's carved in stone; you can tweak your rates until you find the sweet spot between how much you'd like to earn and how much people are actually willing to pay.

Who's It For?

Caregiving is best suited for those who are patient, kind and sensitive; those who are skilled at picking up on other peoples' subtle cues. They're confident in their abilities and they take initiative whenever they see that something needs to be done. They are quick to make a decision when it's called for, and they have excellent judgment. The best caregivers are those who are

---

7   Accessed on July 7, 2016.

not in it just to make money. They are passionate about the art of caregiving.

Although most caregiving roles have traditionally been filled by women, more men are getting into it, especially in the realm of elder care. As our population ages (remember, ten thousand baby boomers turning 65 every single day, and life expectancy on the rise!), even more caregiving opportunities are going to open up for women *and* men in the years ahead.

Getting Started

To get started as a caregiver, you can advertise your services in the local newspaper's classified ads and on community bulletin boards. You can use good old-fashioned networking by telling everyone you know that you're looking for caregiving gigs. You can go through a state or local agency that administers early childhood, disability, in-home health, respite, hospice or aging programs. Or you can use one of the many online avenues for connecting with potential clients.

"Darla" took the path of partnering with an agency, and it worked out beautifully for her. Throughout her 33-year career as a pediatric registered nurse, Darla poured her heart and soul into tending to her little patients. Even though she loved being a professional caregiver, Darla was excited about the next stage of her life: retirement. She and her husband Ray had long been planning a road trip around the country in their RV, visiting America's national parks and stopping to see friends and family along the way.

But only a week after Darla's retirement party and ten days before they were set to leave, Ray was diagnosed with cancer.

The good news was that his prognosis was excellent. The cancer had been caught early and was treatable. The bad news was that they would have to delay their long-anticipated vacation for several months while Ray underwent treatment.

Darla started looking for ways to pass the time while she and Ray waited for the doctors to give them the green light to start their trip. On a morning coffee date with one of her former nursing colleagues, Darla shared her wish to find something to do on the days when Ray didn't have treatment. It was then that her friend told her about a new opportunity coming to their town. Their community's social services department had just received a grant to launch a pilot program providing in-home care for mildly-ill children.

"It's for when a kiddo has the chicken pox or the flu and can't go to school or day care," the friend said. "They're looking for nurses who will go into the homes and stay with the children so the parents don't have to take off work. It's right up your alley, Darla. With all your experience, they'll hire you in a heartbeat. And it's flexible, too; you get to choose when you want to work so you'll always get to be with Ray on treatment days. Look, here's the project coordinator's phone number. Give her a call and see what you think."

Darla made the call that same day, and thus began a wonderful new chapter in her life. Not only did she get to continue applying her amazing caregiving skills to helping children and families in a new and interesting way, but she also made a nice amount of money—$3,600, to be exact—by being an on-call, in-home caregiver a few days a month. The money came in very handy once she and Ray finally hit the road. They were able to extend their trip by several weeks and visit even more scenic places than they'd planned originally.

And when they returned home, Darla went right back to work with the child care program. She loves the flexibility of being able to pick and choose when she'll work. She loves doing something so meaningful with her time. And she *really* loves bringing in that extra money. She and Ray are now saving up for their next trip: a Mediterranean cruise funded entirely by ear infections, tonsillitis, influenza and pink eye.

And then there's "Ellen," a retired school teacher who hooked up with an agency that places assistants in the homes of seniors to help them with light house cleaning, meal prep, personal care and the like. She works as much or as little as she wants, usually doing three six-hour shifts every week at $18 per hour. She had to get certified in CPR and complete a class sponsored by the agency, but that was all it took to begin earning money as a caregiver.

That's how Darla and Ellen got started. But there's another option—technology—which allows you to take control and put yourself and your skills out there big time, and on your own terms.

Care.com

According to its website, Care.com is "the world's largest online destination for care. We connect families with great caregivers and caring companies to help you be there for the ones you love." In other words, the site links people who are looking for a caregiver with care providers in several categories: child care, senior care, pet care and housekeeping. Within those categories are subcategories like tutoring, assisted living, transportation, errands and odd jobs, and much more. Whether you're looking for these services or providing them, Care.com is an efficient one-stop resource.

Let's say you want to provide occasional child care services in your zip code. All you have to do is create an account on Care.com. It's free for a basic membership. You'll simply type in your personal information such as address, email, phone number and date of birth. You'll be asked if you agree to submit to background checks by various third party entities. Then you'll be taken to a page where you can declare your hourly rate, set the types of payments you want to receive (cash, electronic payments, checks), establish how many miles from home you're willing to travel, how many kids you are comfortable watching at one time and the age group you prefer, and whether you're interested in working with sick children and/or children with special needs. You'll write a short bio describing yourself and highlighting your skills and experience. Then you'll upload a selfie photo, and *voila!* You're all set to receive interview requests and job offers from families, and also to apply for any child care gigs posted for your area.

———————◆———————

Another website for connecting child care providers and families is www.SitterCity.com. It operates in much the same way as Care.com. Take a look each of them and see which one has the most job listings in your community. Or sign up for both and double your chances of getting hired.

———————◆———————

If you want to, you can pay a fee to become a premium member of Care.com. The profiles of premium members are highlighted and have better placement in the search result rankings (meaning potential clients will see premium profiles first). You also get early notifications of new job listings. And speaking of notifications, Care.com has an app you can download to your smart phone so you can get immediate announcements of new job listings wherever you happen to be. That way you'll never miss out on an opportunity to make a few bucks.

The procedure for signing up to provide other kinds of services through Care.com is the same as signing up to be a child care provider. And just like on most online job boards, your clients will rate you according their satisfaction with the services you provided. With a professional-looking profile and excellent customer ratings, you can create a very effective "storefront" for your services through this platform and conceivably work whenever you want.

Rover.com

I have a friend, "Dora," who works full-time, mostly from home. She has some flexibility built into her day and she really loves dogs, so she started a dog walking/dog sitting business. Dora has three dogs she walks every morning, plus she regularly boards a couple more in her home when their pet parents travel, which happens frequently. Her house and yard are tiny so she will only keep smaller pets; she is very particular about the type and size of dog she works with. Her clients are extremely grateful to be able to drop off their dogs at Dora's house instead of an impersonal kennel on their way out of town. They know their beloved pets will receive Dora's undivided attention for the duration of their stay. In fact, because she has bonded so deeply with her clients' pooches, Dora says she doesn't need a dog of her own. Not only does she save money on pet food, grooming and vet bills by taking care of other peoples' dogs, but she also makes money just by spending time with her furry friends. Dora earns anywhere from $75 to $200 a week doing something she loves.

Oh, and did I mention that Dora is 72-years old and this is her main source of exercise and activity?

If you're an animal lover like Dora, you can start making money right away by being a pet sitter, boarder or dog walker through Rover.com, which bills itself as "the nation's largest network of dog sitters." There are pet parents hiring caring Rover.com providers in thousands of locations across the country today, so why not get in on the action? Pet care is something you can do as infrequently or as often as you want without making a major investment in time or money.

The procedure for becoming a pet care provider through Rover.com is very similar to that of becoming a provider on Care.com. You create a profile and indicate the types of service(s) you want to provide (boarding, house or pet sitting, day care, drop-ins, dog walking); information about the types of pets you're willing to work with (size range and number of dogs); and your rates. You upload some photos of yourself and the area in and around your home where pets will be kept if you're doing in-home boarding or day care, and you'll agree to undergo a background check. The fine folks at Rover.com will review you application to see if you qualify, a process that takes about a week to complete. As soon as you're approved, your profile will appear on Rover.com and you will start receiving interview and service requests from pet parents in your area.

According to the website, you can earn as much as $1,000 a month via Rover.com. Clients pay you electronically through the Rover site. You keep 80-percent of the fee and Rover gets 20-percent to keep the enterprise going.

Opportunity Snapshot: Caregiving

Pros: Free and easy to get started; flexible hours; work as much or as little as you like

Cons: Irregular pay; lots of competition

Best fit for: People who are nurturing, patient and sensitive; those with very good judgment; people who truly enjoy helping others

Tech Savvy Scale: 2—requires use of a computer, a smart phone and optional apps

---

Further Exploration:

- If you'd like to set yourself apart from the pack by becoming a certified caregiver, visit the American Caregiver Association website at www. AmericanCaregiverAssociation.org. There you'll find training, certification and support for starting your own caregiving business or for working in a care facility.

- Another avenue for linking with dog owners who are seeking quality care for their pets is www.DogVacay. com. The competition here doesn't seem to be as arduous as it is on Rover.com—at least for many cities—so it might be worth looking into.

Meet Archie: Reaching Backward in Order to Move Forward

You've probably noticed by now that one of the main themes woven throughout this book is that you can bring in extra money using skills and connections you already have. You're not required to reinvent the wheel here unless you want to.

For example, I know one gentleman, "Archie," who was a very successful marketing executive for 25-plus years. Archie retired about a decade ago, but to this day he maintains a consulting company catering solely to three of his best and most congenial long-time clients. He will travel, attend conferences on his clients' behalf, connect them to vendors… all the stuff he still gets a kick out of doing. He has basically continued doing the activities he enjoyed the most during his career and left the grunt work behind. Archie has steadily made $15,000 to $30,000 a year working only 20 to 30 hours a month.

I guess what I am trying to say is, if you have a skill you enjoy using and you already have connections in that market, look for a way to leverage those skills and connections. The chances are good that if you have developed a positive, long standing relationship with a client, they would probably rather have you continue working with them in a limited capacity than lose you altogether.

So create a proposal for how you might move forward together and present it to them. You never know. The two of you might be able to work out an arrangement that benefits both of you for years to come.

CHAPTER 9:

MORE SERVICES YOU CAN PROVIDE AROUND TOWN

The following are some additional ways you can offer your assistance to the people in your community and make a little extra cash on the side. These activities don't require much in the way of technology, and again, they're flexible. You can work a little or a lot, and it doesn't take a lot of time or effort to get started.

Tutoring and Lessons

Teachers, retired teachers or subject matter experts can generate a nice income on the side as private tutors. You can either market yourself via Care.com and other online platforms or strike out on your own and promote your tutoring business yourself. It requires a little more legwork to self-promote than it does to fill out an online profile, but it's doable if you go about it strategically. Plus you'll get to keep all your earnings rather than splitting them with the online job board.

Here are a few ideas for tutoring or offering lessons:

- Helping students with academic subjects
- Teaching a foreign language
- Art or craft lessons
- Music lessons
- Sports techniques (I know of a former college softball pitcher who gives pitching lessons to girls around town. She makes a couple thousand dollars every spring)

To get started in this rewarding work, create a resume highlighting the subject(s) you wish to teach as well as your relevant experience and qualifications. Remember, Microsoft Word has free templates you can use to make a professional-looking resume. If you're wanting to tutor academics, visit area schools and see if they need tutoring in their before- or after-school programs. Call every teacher you know to ask if they have any students who might benefit from your services, and if so, ask them to refer the kids' parents to you. Attend PTA meetings and hand out your résumé. And if you know families who homeschool, contact them and see if they or any of their homeschooling friends could use your assistance.

I heard of one guy, "Rich," who took an interesting approach to tutoring by specializing in helping a particular category of pupil: the student athlete. Back when Rich was a young man attending university on a football scholarship, he'd struggled academically to the point where he was in danger of losing his scholarship. In a last ditch effort to save Rich's college career, his coach hooked him up with a tutor; a retired school teacher named "Edna." Rich and Edna met in the library three days a week for two semesters to work on his assignments. Thanks to Edna's skill and dedication—and Rich's determination to succeed—he was able to bring up his grades and maintain them. Ultimately he graduated from college and became a sports writer.

Upon his retirement from the newspaper business, Rich reached out to all the high school coaches in his town and offered to tutor any student athletes who were struggling with reading and/or writing. They all jumped at the offer and sent a steady stream of kids his way. Whenever a youngster's parents couldn't afford to pay for the sessions, the athletic booster club picked up the tab. In some cases Rich donated the money right back to the club or waived the fee entirely. For him, it was mostly about giving back. It was his way of thanking Edna for salvaging his college education.

It's cool if you want to be like Rich and donate your services to help young people succeed academically. But if you're wanting to make money through tutoring, you can definitely fulfill that mission too. According to PayScale.com, the average hourly rate for tutors nationwide is $17. However, it's possible to earn much more than that in some locales, where private tutors receive up to $50 an hour.

Here's hoping you live in one of those places!

Translation and Interpretation

According to the U.S. Bureau of Labor Statistics, the need for translation and interpretation services is on the rise and not showing signs of letting up anytime soon, with translators and interpreters earning an average of $21 per hour.[8] So if you are fluent in more than one language, you may be able to earn money as a translator or interpreter in your community. Schools, hospitals and other health care settings, social services agencies, courts, jails and police departments all have a need for translators and interpreters at one point or another. Interpreting and translating for people in these settings is a huge responsibility and is extremely rewarding.

---◆---

Interpreters versus Translators: What's the Difference?
Interpreters work with spoken communications and sign language.
Translators deal strictly with written communications.

---◆---

A friend of mine, "Gail," told me a great story about how an interpreter made a big difference for one family in need. Gail used to be the resident manager of a Ronald McDonald House, which are low-cost accommodations located near hospitals where the families of seriously ill children can stay while their child receives treatment. No one is ever turned away from one of these houses for an inability to pay. Many years ago, a family

---

8   http://www.bls.gov/ooh/media-and-communication/interpreters-and-translators.htm, accessed July 13, 2016.

from Haiti came to stay at the Ronald McDonald House Gail managed when their child was admitted to the hospital for life-saving surgery. Gail and her staff were eager to help the family feel at home, but there was one little problem: a major language barrier. They didn't speak a word of English and nobody on staff spoke Creole, plus the intake paperwork was in English and Spanish only. There was no way to communicate with the already stressed out family, who by now had no idea what was happening to them.

Gail called the hospital's social work department and asked if they knew of any Creole speakers who could come to the House and interpret the intake process. They did... a retired nurse originally from Haiti had done some translation and interpretation for them in the past. Long story short, Gail called the woman and she was at the House within the hour. When she greeted the family in Creole, they burst into tears. They were no longer alone. The nurse interpreted and translated for that family for the duration of their stay, and Gail and the social worker arranged for the hospital foundation to pay for her services.

The main thing to remember about doing this kind of work is that you must have native-level fluency in at least two languages. There are various certifications out there to prove your proficiency. I recommend that you check into earning certification before you put yourself out there as an interpreter/translator.

Mystery Shopper

You know how I'm always saying that if you want to earn extra cash, you should try to make money doing something you enjoy? Well, this money-making opportunity is for those of you with a passion for shopping. You really can earn money by hanging out in your favorite stores as a mystery shopper. Here's how it works: businesses hire independent contractors (the mystery shoppers) to go into their establishments and perform certain tasks to check the quality of the customer experience, or to analyze other aspects of the operation. In most cases the shopper is expected to remain anonymous while they're in the store. It's kind of like being a secret agent but without the poison dart pen.

For example, a hospitality management company might hire you to assess employee integrity by going to their hotel bar, ordering a drink and observing how the bartender pours and rings up your purchase, as well as how he/she treats a specified number of other patrons. You report on your experience to the company to get reimbursed for your purchase and they give you an additional $30 for your trouble. Or an auto maintenance chain might hire you to take your car in for an oil change so you can assess the quality of the service. Afterward you're reimbursed for the oil change and given an additional $20 for your time. My research shows that the pay for mystery shopping gigs varies widely; you can earn anywhere between $5 and $150 depending on the complexity of the particular job.

To get started in this fun and potentially lucrative activity, log on to the website for the Mystery Shopping Providers Association of North America (MSPA-NA) at www.mspa-na.org and click on "Independent Contractors." You'll be prompted to join the association (the basic membership is free) and create a profile. Once you've done that you'll have access to the MSPA-NA's database of companies with legitimate mystery shopping opportunities. You have the option of upgrading to a paid membership to get priority access to MSPA-NA's job listings, webinars and training.

I'd be remiss if I didn't mention that the mystery shopping field is ripe for exploitation and scams. Avoid any promoters that charge you a fee to access their database of jobs. No legitimate mystery shopping promoter will make you pay to get "certified," guarantee you a job, or try to get you to cash a check or wire money to someone on their behalf. As always, trust your gut. Walk away if you have any doubts about the authenticity of the opportunity.

Furniture Delivery and Assembly

No matter how simple Ikea tries to make their instructions for furniture assembly, many of their customers are still not going to be able to decipher them… or aren't interested in even trying. Millions of people buy unassembled goods online these days, too, so if you enjoy following directions and working with your hands, furniture assembly might be a good sideline for you. And if you're willing to do deliveries AND set up the goods, this kind of work could become a real cash cow.

Think about the types of people who would most likely use a delivery and assembly service. Seniors, apartment dwellers, people with disabilities, single parents… they could all benefit from having a reliable delivery and assembly person in their back pocket. The furniture stores themselves (especially smaller mom-and-pop stores) would probably love to have a dependable backup to fill in for sick employees, or to help out during the holidays. So do a little targeted advertising and a lot of networking, and see if you can hammer out an opportunity or two for yourself.

Opportunity Snapshot: More Services Around Town

Pros: Most are free and easy to get started; flexible hours; work as much or as little as you like; some gigs pay pretty well

Cons: Irregular pay; lots of competition; may require extensive self-promotion

Best fit for: People with an open mind and a sense of humor; people who truly enjoy helping others

Tech Savvy Scale: 2—may require use of a computer and a smart phone

---

Further Exploration:

- For information about becoming an interpreter in the court system, visit the National Center for State Courts at www.ncsc.org. Under the "Education & Careers" tab, choose "State Interpreter Certification."
- If you'd like to look into doing tutoring online rather than face-to-face, visit www.tutor.com and click "Become a Tutor."

SELLING GOODS

CHAPTER 10:

SELLING ONLINE

B ack in the day you'd have to go to a sleazy pawn shop or have a yard sale if you wanted to make money selling your stuff. Yard sales in particular were a time consuming project. You'd have to clean up all the merchandise, mark each piece with a price, advertise your sale in the newspaper, go to the bank and get a bunch of change, and cross your fingers that it wouldn't rain. You'd get up early on the day of your sale, set up everything and post signs around the neighborhood. A lot of people you don't know would come over and dig through your stuff, not-so-subtly judging its quality (and your taste) and trying to haggle with you over the prices. Exhausted at the end of the day, you'd take all the unsold merchandise back inside again and try to figure out what to do with it. It was not a relaxing way to spend your weekend.

But thanks to the internet you can now sell items online quickly and securely, any time of the day or night and to people near or far. You can sell new things, used things, things you've made. You can sell a single item or thousands of them, all with the click of a mouse.

How Much Can You Earn?

It depends on what you're selling and how much time you're willing to invest in posting items, marketing them properly and fulfilling the orders. Some individuals make thousands of dollars a month selling online; others make pocket change. It's entirely up to you. Keep in mind that you'll have to pay for packaging and shipping, but you can factor that into the price you set for your merchandise.

Who's It For?

Online selling is a good fit for people who like using computers and digital cameras, which are necessary for taking pictures of your merchandise. You should enjoy doing research into the kinds of merchandise most likely to sell via the various e-commerce platforms. You'll also need to conduct research into the value of your items so you can price them appropriately.

The best online sellers are skilled at marketing and persuasion. They work hard to make their online storefronts and each individual listing look as professional as they possibly can. They take the time to ensure that their item descriptions are grammatically correct and spell-checked. They are completely honest when describing their merchandise, and they are dedicated to providing outstanding customer service so they can earn positive reviews and maintain high ratings.

Getting Started

Your first stop on the road to online selling should be at PayPal.com. PayPal is an online payment system that allows people all over the world to do business with one another. Many venues for online selling require that you have a PayPal account for electronically transferring the proceeds of your sales directly from the buyer's account to yours. It's secure, it's fast, and the fees to use the service are reasonable. PayPal is not only for selling stuff online; you can use it in just about any sales scenario. For instance, when you open one of their business accounts you can accept credit card payments in person using a PayPal-issued card reader device, which links to your smart phone or tablet.

To open a PayPal account for business or personal use, go to www.PayPal.com and click "Sign Up." Follow the simple prompts from there. You'll be ready to accept electronic payments in minutes.

Selling on Ebay.com

Founded in 1995, Ebay was first to the e-commerce party, and it's still the leader in online consumer-to-consumer selling. Here you can peddle anything from household goods and jewelry to collectibles and cars. You can auction off your item to the highest bidder or simply offer it for sale at a fixed price. I have found Ebay to be great for things that you can ship easily, as it gives you access to a wide national or even an international audience. It is also good for higher-priced items. I know many people who have bought cars there. My mother-in-law even bought a house on Ebay. My father, who was an optometrist, bought specialized equipment for over $100,000 there at substantial discounts. He also sold equipment there, and we unloaded our school musical instruments on Ebay when we were done with them.

In most cases it's free to list an item on Ebay (unless you want one of their optional upgrades), but they will take a cut of the proceeds if your item sells. The percentage of that cut varies depending on the merchandise type, whether you're running an auction or a fixed-price sale, and the item's final selling price. In most cases the fee is around ten percent. And since buyers' payments are processed through PayPal, you'll be charged a small fee by them as well.

It's easy to list an item on Ebay. You'll begin by logging on to the site and opening a seller account, which you will then link to your PayPal account (no worries; Ebay makes this simple). Now decide what you want to sell. Again, this should be easy. Look around the room you're sitting in and you can probably find something of value that you'd like to unload. A book, a vase, the watch you never wear anymore, a baseball signed by Mickey Mantle (actually, I'll buy that from you right now!) … you can offer any of them for sale on Ebay. Do some internet research to see how much similar items are selling for on Ebay and elsewhere. Once you decide on a price, add in the cost of packaging materials and shipping. Now you can offer the item with "free shipping," which is more attractive to buyers.

Next you'll create your listing, the centerpiece of which will be photographs of your item. Ebay lets you post several photos at no charge, so take advantage of that. Shoot lots of clear pictures showing the item from different angles and a variety of distances. If your merchandise has any dents or dings, don't try to hide them. You want potential customers to be fully informed about what they're buying; first of all because it's the right thing to do, and second of all because they'll give you terrible ratings if they feel you've ripped them off. So photograph the damage and also mention it in your description along with all the positive things you want to say about the item. Be honest and be thorough. Decide if you want your sale to be an auction or fixed price, upload your photos, finish typing in your sales pitch—Ebay gives you good examples from other listings that you can use as references—and hit the button to launch your sale.

Traffic on e-commerce websites is usually higher on weekends, so try posting your item for ten days beginning on a Thursday. That way your listing will appear on two consecutive weekends, giving it more visibility.

When your item sells and the buyer's payment clears (Ebay and PayPal will let you know when that happens) you'll prepare the item for shipping. Ebay will generate a packing slip and an address label for you. All you have to do is print them out, package your item carefully and professionally, and take it to the shipper of your choice.

If your item doesn't sell you can always list it again, or try offering a different item. Remember, you're not limited to only selling the stuff lying around your house. You can scour yard sales, thrift shops, auctions and department store clearance bins for great deals and then sell them on Ebay for a profit. Over time you'll develop an eye for what people want. And if you can create a niche for yourself, even better. For example, I heard about a prolific hobby quilter who started selling her leftover fabric on Ebay and quickly generated a following among quilters looking for bargain material. When her local quilt shop went out of business, she and her husband bought some of the inventory dirt cheap and listed it for sale on Ebay... fabric, thread, pattern books, batting, scissors, rotary cutters and the like. She made enough profit to buy herself the sewing machine of her dreams.

What about you? Do you have a hobby you could build upon in the same way? If you make bird houses, you could create kits and sell them. You could do the same with jewelry, knitting, crocheting, scrapbooking, kite-making... virtually any kind of art or craft could generate success similar to that experienced by our quilter friend.

And speaking of arts and crafts...

Selling on Etsy.com

Etsy has become an extremely popular forum for buying and selling hand-made and vintage merchandise, as well as craft supplies and tools. There you can find items such as:

- Clothing and accessories
- Home décor
- Jewelry
- Wedding apparel, decorations and supplies
- Craft supplies, including but not limited to materials for making jewelry, rugs, cakes, soap, ceramics, doll houses, etc.

In 2015 alone, Etsy boasted 24 million buyers who spent over $2.3 billion on their platform. Tapping into this vast market is easy and inexpensive. You simply use the Etsy website to open a customizable "shop" where you can offer your wares for sale. There are no monthly fees to keep your shop open. Instead you'll be charged a small amount for each listing (at the time of this writing it's 20 cents) and when your item sells Etsy will take out a transaction fee and a payment processing fee, which together are around seven percent of the sale price. In exchange for that, you get to access the Etsy platform, support, educational materials, and tons of tools to maximize your earning potential.

Opening an Etsy shop is similar to listing an item on Ebay. You'll create an account; name your virtual shop and design it with the help of free templates; upload photos, videos and descriptions of your items and register your banking information so you can pay and be paid.

Remember, Etsy is ONLY for selling vintage items that are at least 20 years old, handmade items, and craft supplies. For everything else, there's good ol' Amazon.com.

Selling on Amazon.com

Selling stuff to Amazon's tens of millions of customers is pretty much the same as selling on Ebay or Etsy. Here you can offer new, used and refurbished items in 20 categories, including collectibles, art, clothing, electronics, books, toys, etc. You start by opening a seller's account. If you're going to be offering more than 40 items a month, you'll open a "professional" account and be charged a flat monthly fee (right now that's $39.99). If you're going to be listing less than 40 items monthly, you'll open an "individual" account and pay a small fee for each listing you post (right now that's 99 cents per listing). You'll photograph your items, create product descriptions, and upload them. Like I said, it's the same as the other platforms, but with one notable exception: the opportunity to utilize Amazon's "Fulfilled by Amazon" (FBA) program.

With FBA, you box up all the stuff you want to sell, ship it to Amazon, list the items for sale and Amazon takes it from there. They'll warehouse your merchandise until it sells, and then they'll fulfill the order: they pick it from the shelves, package it, ship it, and handle any customer service issues that arise. It's a great time saver, and you don't have to mess with the hassle of packing and shipping, except for that original shipment to Amazon, of course. FBA was originally created for sellers with huge inventories, but anyone can use it. The fees vary depending on how much space your items take up in the warehouse and how much it costs to package and ship them. You can learn the details at www.amazon.com/fba.

Opportunity Snapshot: Selling Online

Pros: Inexpensive or free to get started; you can manage your business from anywhere as long as there's an internet connection

Cons: Income is 100-percent dependent on sales; very competitive markets unless you can fill a specialized niche

Best Fit For: People who want to earn money from home; those with an entrepreneurial spirit who enjoy the art of the deal

Tech Savvy Scale: 3—requires use of a computer and digital camera as well as being able to work within the parameters of your chosen e-commerce website

---

Further Exploration:

Here are a few more e-commerce sites worth checking out:

- www.Swappa.com (a very popular site for buying/selling gently-used mobile devices; no fee for sellers!)

- www.Bonanza.com (this site has an affiliate program that they say "offers generous referral rates, plus tools to build your audience and reduce work.")

- www.Ebid.net (free listings, very low sales fee of just 3 percent, and support from real live human beings.)

Jolene, the Yard Sale Queen

Jolene has always loved three things beyond all else: God, her family, and shopping. But Jolene wasn't the kind of shopper who strolled around a nice cool mall every weekend. She was the kind of shopper who got up at the crack of dawn on Saturday morning, grabbed a Thermos™ full of hot coffee, fired up the minivan and headed to her first yard sale of the day. Jolene had spent the evening before scouring the classified ad section of the newspaper, circling the addresses for what she considered to be the most promising yard sales of the upcoming weekend. At sunrise the next day she'd take to the road and hit them all.

It was at one of those sales that Jolene came up with the perfect money-making opportunity for her. The couple holding this particular sale clearly had no idea what they were doing. Most of the items weren't marked with a price, so people had to chase them around asking, "How much is this? How much is this?" The majority of their merchandise was dusty; it looked as if they'd simply dragged everything down from the attic at the last minute and dumped it on the lawn. They ran out of change within half an hour, so the line of people trying to pay for their purchases kept growing longer and longer. Some folks simply gave up and left without buying anything at all.

Jolene and a neighbor stood together off to the side, shaking their heads and watching the chaos unfold.

"Their first mistake was putting their checkout table over there in the corner. It creates a bottleneck," Jolene said. "Their second mistake was piling so much stuff into boxes. Nobody can see what's there. And why in the world don't they have a calculator next to the money box? It's crazy!"

"Yep, it's a mess all right. You know, they should've hired you to run their sale," the neighbor chuckled. "Then they wouldn't have all these problems. Nobody knows more about yard sales than you do."

It was true: nobody knew yard sales like Jolene. Nobody loved them more, either. Yard sales were her passion. This got Jolene thinking: *what if she could make money helping people put on great yard sales?* She could go to their houses in advance, organize all their stuff and plan the physical layout of the sale. She'd mark all the merchandise and handle all the advertising. She'd show up on the day of the sale to set up and run the whole thing. At the end of the day she'd take 40-percent of the proceeds.

And that's exactly what she did. Eventually Jolene became known throughout her small Midwestern city as the Yard Sale Queen. Not only did she organize sales for people at their homes, but for an extra 10 percent she would transport the items to her house and hold the sale there, making the entire process hassle-free for her clients.

As technology changed, so did Jolene's business. With the advent of Ebay and other online selling platforms, she began offering merchandise online. With help from her kids (and later, her grandkids) she'd pick up the items from the client's home, research them to see what they were worth, list them for sale online and manage the whole process in exchange for 50-percent of the proceeds. When clients had something in their basement that wasn't marketable or was hard to ship—such as used clothing or old furniture—Jolene would pick up the items, donate them to Goodwill and claim the tax deduction. She'd clean out the rest of the client's basement and charge a junk removal fee to haul off any additional unwanted items to the dump. On most of these jobs Jolene made several hundred to several thousand dollars, which helped her and her husband Joe save up for a secure retirement.

Last year Jolene stepped aside and passed the Yard Sale Queen crown to her daughter, Arlene, who plans to carry on the family tradition—and beef up her family's savings account—for many more years to come.

CHAPTER 11:

SELLING IN YOUR COMMUNITY

There are a couple of benefits to selling things to the folks in your community rather than selling to strangers online. First, you don't have the hassle of packing and shipping. You simply hand the merchandise directly to its new owner and collect your money. Second, you get to meet new people. You might not consider this a benefit if you're shy or an introvert, but for the more gregarious among us, it's a happy perk. Third, you can sell a wider variety of stuff close to home than you can online. Some things are difficult or even impossible to ship, including but not limited to bulky furniture, live plants and many fresh food items. The people in your community may be your only option for unloading these types of merchandise. It's also the best way to sell something the buyer may want to inspect before purchasing it, either to make sure it works or to confirm that it's the right size, color, etc.

How Much Can You Earn?

Like any sales endeavor, your earnings depend on how many items you're able to sell and for how much. Again, the cool thing about selling in person directly to a buyer is that you don't have to mess with or pay for packaging and shipping. You get to keep more of what you make.

Who's It For?

Selling directly to consumers is a good fit for people who enjoy doing research into which items are most popular and how much they're worth. The best salespeople are persuasive and like to market their merchandise. They enjoy getting out of the house and meeting people face-to-face. They have a thick skin; they are not easily deterred by rejection. They simply shake it off and move on to the next prospect.

Getting Started

The hardest part of selling items in your community may be deciding what you're going to sell. There are so many possibilities that it may be tough to choose. As problems go, I'd say this is a pretty good one to have!

If you're going to be selling directly to buyers I strongly encourage you to pick a product you're passionate about; a product you yourself enjoy using or owning. When you care about the items you're selling, you will naturally be more knowledgeable and enthusiastic about them. Enthusiasm is contagious. Think about the last time you interacted with a salesperson. If they were excited about what they were selling, chances are you became excited about it, too. But if they were indifferent, it's likely that you didn't care about it either. People who don't care about things simply don't buy them. So do yourself, your customers and your bank account a favor and sell something you like.

Just as with online sales, it's a good idea to open a PayPal account before you begin selling because it will give you access to a credit card reader. Having a card reader will make it possible for you to accept another form of payment in addition to cash. Cashless transactions are the norm these days. Don't miss out on a sale because you only take cash. You want to make it super easy for people to give you their money.

Once you know what you're selling and have the ability to accept payments, it's time to decide where you're going to sell your goods. The following are only a few of the interesting places where you can connect with buyers in your community.

Selling via Craigslist.org and Facebook's Swap-N-Shop

You may wonder why I've included Craigslist and Facebook here rather than putting them in the previous chapter about online selling. The reason is that although Craigslist and Facebook are internet sites, they are intended to link you with *local* buyers, not remote ones. The same is true of your newspaper's online classified ads. I guess you could say that these are "hybrids" of online and face-to-face marketing.

Let's begin with Craigslist, the modern day equivalent of the old-fashioned newspaper ad. You can sell new or used items via this forum, and best of all, it's free. Craigslist is great for getting rid of stuff from around the house... stuff you need a truck to pick up or deliver, like appliances, furniture, and miscellaneous junk. It's also good for things that people want to inspect before buying to make sure they work.

All you have to do is visit Craigslist.org and click on your state and city (or region) to get started. You'll be taken to your localized page. Click on the "post to classifieds" button in the upper left hand corner and you're off to the races. You'll be prompted to pick your item's category (cars, clothes, jewelry, RVs, sporting goods, event tickets, cell phones, bikes, you name it) and you'll then be taken to the page where you'll compose your ad.

By now you will have done research into what your item is worth, and you'll remember to employ all the tips for making a good online ad: make it honest, make it descriptive, and make it professional (in other words, spell-check it and DON'T USE ALL CAPITAL LETTERS or silly symbols). You'll get to choose whether you want potential buyers to contact you by email, phone and/or text. You'll take some quality photos of your item from a variety of angles and perspectives. As of right now, Craigslist lets you post a whopping 24 pictures to each ad, so fire away. Upload your best shot first, as it will be your ad's featured photo. Then you'll proofread your draft and publish it. Your ad will go live immediately. It'll stay online for 45 days or until you take it down. You can renew your listing as many times as you want if your item doesn't sell right away.

You can also offer merchandise for sale within your community via Facebook. Start by checking Facebook to see if there is a "Swap-N-Shop" group near you. For example, I live in Baltimore so I logged on to Facebook and did a search for "Baltimore Swap Shop." Bingo! Two different groups popped up; one of them has almost 5,000 members. Most of the time these groups have closed memberships, meaning you'll have to request permission to join. It's easy to do and it's free; you just click on the "Join Group" button. Once the page administrators have approved your membership you can start making posts to the page. These posts will only be seen by the group's members.

If there is no Swap Shop group serving your locality, don't despair. Be a pioneer and start one. Facebook makes it easy. Just go to their Help Center and search "How Do I Create a Group?" for step-by-step instructions.

Safety First!

While most face-to-face interactions that originate on sites like Craigslist and Facebook end well, there are some unfortunate instances in which they did not. Craigslist has published a number of tips for protecting yourself when meeting up with potential buyers whom you don't know. Check them out at www.craigslist.org/about/safety.

Selling at Pawn Shops

If the first word that comes to mind when you think of pawn shops is "sleazy," you are not alone. Pawn shops are often located in the roughest part of town, and they have a reputation for being the place where desperate people go to get quick cash to solve whatever horrendous problem they're having that day.

But there's more to pawn shops than that. You don't have to be desperate to sell something in one, and there are some really nice and interesting pawn shops across America where people go to purchase great merchandise—I'm thinking of Miami in particular, where a few of the better shops even have fresh flowers, piped-in classical music and chandeliers hanging from the ceilings.

There are two ways to get money at a pawn shop: selling an item outright or offering an item as collateral in exchange for a loan. You get the item back if you repay the loan on time. For the purposes of this book we're going to stick with selling items outright.

The secrets for successful pawn shop selling are (a) offering the right kind of item, (b) knowing exactly what it is worth, (c) finding the best shop for that item, and (d) keeping your head during negotiations. The right kind of item is something that'll be relatively easy for the pawn dealer to pass along to a willing buyer, namely:

- Quality jewelry, especially gold and platinum
- Power tools
- Newer high-end electronics

Your strategy goes something like this: do your research so you understand *exactly* what the merchandise is worth. Also research your area pawn shops by running them through the local Better Business Bureau website. Decide on the minimum amount you're willing to accept for the item, and consider that amount carved in stone, at least for today. Clean and/or repair the merchandise so it looks its absolute best.

Once at the pawn shop, do not tell the dealer how much you paid for the item or give them any indication of how much you want for it. Instead, simply show it to them and ask how much they're willing to give you for it. Feel free to negotiate (all the while keeping your cool and maintaining your bottom dollar) and also feel free to leave and go on to the next shop if you're not satisfied with the offer. Rinse and repeat until you get the offer you're looking for. And if it doesn't work out, no sweat. You have plenty of other options.

Selling at Consignment Shops

Consignment shops are places where people bring in merchandise and allow the store owner to sell it on their behalf for a percentage of the sales price. For example, let's say your son has outgrown his bike. You take it to the consignment shop for a set period of time (usually 30-, 60- or 90-days) and either set a price in collaboration with the shop owner or have the shop owner set the price. If the bike sells, you split the proceeds according to the store's policy. If it doesn't sell you can either lower the price and try again or pick it up and take it home.

There are a couple of benefits to selling on consignment. The first is that you maintain ownership of the merchandise until somebody buys it or until you pick it up. The second is that you don't have to spend any time or energy on the act of selling; the store handles all that. The downfall is that you will pay a fairly hefty commission to the shop. But if you're the kind of person who dislikes haggling with potential buyers or simply wants to take a hands-off approach to the sales process, you might prefer to sell your goods this way.

Selling at Flea Markets

Flea markets are a staple in many communities, especially in the summer months when outdoor bazaars and farmer's markets pop up in towns all across the country. You can sell merchandise at markets like these on weekends with no long-term commitment. You can even travel from market to market, setting up shop at a new venue in a different town every weekend. Then there are the indoor flea markets that operate year 'round; the kind where you lease a space for a certain period of time (usually a minimum of a month) and you staff it several days a week.

Weekend flea markets in particular are a great example of a money-making venture that's relatively easy to try without making a big initial commitment of time or resources. And if you're the outgoing type, you can have a lot of fun too.

◆

A quick and dirty way to find out if the flea market scene is for you is to hold your next yard sale at one. Just clean out your house, haul the goods to the market, and you're in business. For a minimal space rental fee (probably less than the cost of a newspaper ad) you'll be seen by hundreds of potential customers.

◆

The best thing about flea markets is that almost anything goes. I've seen vendors selling all kinds of things: walking sticks, kitchen scouring pads, replica swords, shell necklaces, freshly baked bread, old vinyl records, orchids, and belts. Antiques, dollar store-style trinkets, local honey, handmade dresses, flags, and beads. Dog collars. Spice blends. T-shirts. Amish cheese. Tools. Stuffed animals. Toiletries. Sometimes people craft the items themselves. Others buy cheap wholesale merchandise and sell it for a markup. Still others go to garage sales or thrift stores and buy individual items they believe they can sell for more at the market. I heard of one retired couple who bought out another vendor's indoor flea market business for $10,000 because the vendor had health problems and couldn't continue. The merchandise had been quite neglected so the couple cleaned everything up. They rearranged the space and added some nice touches here and there to make it look more appealing, more like a little store. They ended up raking in roughly $2,000 in sales *every weekend for six months.*[9]

All it takes to get started in the flea market game is a flea market to go to, your chosen merchandise, a table, some containers to hold your stuff as you transport it to and from the venue, and a vehicle to get you there. A credit card reader will also come in handy, as will a healthy sense of humor. Even if

---

9   Your mileage may vary.

sales aren't what you'd hoped for, you'll likely have a good time taking in the lively cast of characters you'll encounter there.

**Opportunity Snapshot:
Selling Goods in Your Community**

Pros: Inexpensive or free to get started; unlimited sales possibilities

Cons: Income is 100-percent dependent on sales

Best Fit For: People with an entrepreneurial spirit who enjoy the art of the deal; those who like getting out and meeting people

Tech Savvy Scale: 2—may require use of a computer, digital camera and a credit card reader linked to your smart phone.

Further Exploration:

- To find an appraiser near you to help determine the value of a particular item or items, visit the American Society of Appraisers at www.appraisers.org/find-an-appraiser.
- For a list of flea markets across the United States and Canada, visit http://fleamarketzone.com/flea-market-directory/.

ADDITIONAL
INTERESTING GIGS

CHAPTER 12:

BECOMING PART OF THE CROWD

I t used to be that your options were limited if you had a good business idea but needed money to get it off the ground. You could ask your family, friends or the bank for a loan. You could try to attract a venture capitalist or angel investor. Or you could use credit cards to finance your startup (yikes!). The bottom line is that unless your name was Walton or Du Pont, you were pretty much on your own.

And it also used to be that you were on your own if you were a freelance service provider like a writer, a researcher, a graphic artist, etc. It was up to you to find your own gigs and to complete them yourself from start to finish.

But with the advent and evolution of the internet, aspiring entrepreneurs and freelancers are no longer alone unless they want to be. Now, thanks to crowdfunding and crowd working, you can leverage the power of the masses to (1) get money to pursue a business objective through *crowdfunding*, and (2) work on money-making tasks that would have been out of your reach before as a solo worker via *crowd working*. Let's take a look at how each system works.

Crowdfunding

Everybody loves an underdog. So if you're a little guy with an idea for a product or service but need cash to make it happen, head over to Kickstarter.com (or IndieGoGo.com) where there are millions of people willing to donate money to help folks like you get the ball rolling. Kickstarter defines itself as a platform that "helps artists, musicians, filmmakers, designers, and other creators find the resources and support they need to make their ideas a reality." Since its inception in 2009, Kickstarter has helped people launch over 100,000 projects with $2.5 billion in funding from 11 million donors, and it's showing no signs of letting up anytime soon. According to a 2015 article in Forbes magazine, the amount of money generated through crowdfunding will transcend that of venture capital in 2016.[10]

To tap into this revenue stream you have to have a compelling idea for a product or service in one of the project categories that can be funded through Kickstarter:

- Art
- Comics

---

10   http://www.forbes.com/sites/chancebarnett/2015/06/09/trends-show-crowdfunding-to-surpass-vc-in-2016/#14b2bd06444b, accessed July 18, 2016.

- Crafts
- Dance
- Design
- Fashion
- Film and Video
- Food
- Games
- Journalism
- Music
- Photography
- Publishing
- Technology
- Theater

Let's say you have an idea to create a picture book featuring antique steam engines, and you need $5,000 to make that happen. You submit your project idea to the Kickstarter.com team and they give you feedback to improve your proposal's potential for attracting donors. Then you create a project post in which you tell your story, describe the picture book you want to make and why it's different or better than others. You'll tell how much money you are hoping to generate through Kickstarter and how you'll use the funds.

You'll also describe the rewards you'll be giving to donors should the project reach full-funding. For example, for donations of $1 to $5, you could promise to email the donor one of the photos from the book for use as a screensaver for their computer. For people who donate larger amounts, you could pledge to mail them a poster, or include their names in the book's Acknowledgements section, or give them a discount on the book when it comes out... you get the idea. Now you start networking and telling everyone you know about the project—especially your buddies who love antique steam engines—and ask them to make a donation to your Kickstarter campaign. You also ask them to spread the word by telling all *their* steam engine friends about it, too.

———————◆———————

One of the best things about launching a product with funding from Kickstarter or IndieGoGo rather than traditional venture capital is that you retain all rights to the product. Unlike partnering with an investor, you're not selling a stake in the venture... people are essentially donating to make it happen.

———————◆———————

If you reach your goal of $5,000 within the established time frame, Kickstarter will collect money from all the people who pledged funds (they will have entered their credit card information in advance and the money will come out of their accounts automatically) and you'll send them the rewards you promised. Kickstarter will keep a small percentage of the money you raised and deposit the remainder into your bank account. If your goal is not met, the project expires, nobody's card is charged, and you don't have to distribute any rewards. No harm, no foul.

Crowdfunding can be a very effective way of getting a worthwhile project off the ground. Give it a try. What have you got to lose?

Crowd Working

If you enjoy doing small repetitive tasks, crowd working may be for you. Crowd working, also known as micro-working, is gaining steam worldwide as a way for companies to get help completing big jobs made up of lots of little parts that cannot be automated effectively... jobs like testing search results for certain keywords, translating written content from one language to another, data processing, identifying specific information on sets of receipts or images, etc. This is different from freelancing, because although both are part of the crowd, freelancing is generally skilled labor while crowd working is usually more mundane.

These tiny jobs are posted on websites like Mechanical Turk (www.mturk.com), CrowdCloud.com and ClickWorker.com. All you have to do to begin earning money on them is create an account, search through their databases of available tasks and get to work. You may have to prove your abilities before being allowed to work on select gigs, but once you're authorized you'll have access to thousands of money-making opportunities. On Mechanical Turk, these opportunities are called Human Intelligence Tasks, or HITs, because they require an actual human being to do them. Pay is small—usually pennies per HIT—but it can add up if you do it often enough. Some tasks are so mindless you could do them while watching TV, or at least during the commericals.

Another way to earn money through crowd working, especially if you're a creative person, is to log on to websites like 99Designs.com and CrowdSpring.com. On these sites, also called *crowdsourcing* sites, you'll find scores of individuals and companies looking for help creating logos, icons, web designs and other graphics… even people looking for help coming up with a name for their baby. You read the project descriptions (which includes the budget for each one) and create and submit your designs or ideas for consideration. If the client picks yours, you get the money. Some of the gigs posted on these sites pay a fair amount of money (anywhere between $100 and $1,000), but the downside is that competition is fierce and you'll be doing the work with no guarantee that you'll ever be paid for your efforts. If you're OK with that, give these sites a try and see if you can generate some business there.

◆

Opportunity Snapshot: Being Part of the Crowd

Pros: Free to get started; you get to retain ownership of your idea with Kickstarter

Cons: Stiff competition; income varies widely; very low pay for most crowd working

Best Fit For: People who enjoy repetitive tasks; those with an entrepreneurial spirit and good connections

Tech Savvy Scale: 2-4—depends on the task; requires use of a computer and the ability to navigate websites

◆

Further Exploration:

- For step-by-step instructions for creating, posting and managing a project on Kickstarter, see their Creator Handbook at www.kickstarter.com/help/handbook.

- Another place to be part of the "in crowd" is at www. Fiverr.com, where you can establish a virtual storefront and post offers to perform tasks such as "I will create your business logo for $10" or "I will be your web site writer for $50." Buyers then peruse all the offers and reach out to those creators whose profiles they like.

Meet Kay, Who LOVES to Win

If there's anyone who loves to compete, it's "Kay." When she was a young woman, Kay played softball and basketball, earning all-state honors in both sports. As she got older she took up golf… table tennis… billiards… bridge… mahjong… and in each of those pursuits she was a fierce competitor. Kay loves putting her skills up against those of other people. Most of all, *she loves winning*.

And that's why when Kay read an article on the internet about competing for crowdsourcing projects, she couldn't wait to give it a try. Now that she was retired, she had plenty of time to explore interesting opportunities like that. She logged on to CrowdSpring.com, created a profile, and started reading through all the creative contests that were open on the platform that day. There were hundreds of them in categories like logo and web design, banner ads, email templates, illustrations, slogans for t-shirts and coffee mugs, and much more. As a former English teacher, Kay was especially eager to try her hand at one of the "naming" projects where businesses and individuals challenge the crowd to come up with the name of their latest product, their new company, their boat, etc. It's free to submit an idea and if yours is chosen, you win an award of anywhere from $200 to several thousand dollars.

Kay entered dozens of naming contests before her first win: $200 for coming up with the name of a new spa opening in a city across the country. From that moment on she was hooked. Kay has entered hundreds of contests since then and won four of them for an earnings total of $1,200. Entering the crowdsourcing contests keeps her mind sharp and gives her something to do. But most of all it stokes her competitive spirit. It's the thrill of winning that keeps her coming back for more.

CHAPTER 13:

UNCONVENTIONAL MONEY-MAKERS

The ideas presented in this chapter may not appeal to everybody, but hopefully they'll serve as inspiration to those of you who are willing to try something outside the ordinary to make a few bucks. A couple of these activities require quite a bit more from you than the other money-making opportunities we've discussed throughout this book. But as they say, you only live once.

Giving of Yourself… Literally

If you're not scared of needles, you can earn up to $400 a month by **donating your plasma**. Plasma is the clear liquid that is the main ingredient in human blood. It's full of enzymes and antibodies, and it's used to formulate therapies that help people with medical problems like auto-immune and blood clotting disorders.

In order to donate plasma you have to be between the ages of 18 and 65 and free from diseases like HIV and hepatitis. You'll be given a physical exam and your medical history will be taken down before your first donation session to make sure you're eligible. If you're approved, you'll be hooked up to a "plasmapheresis machine" via a needle in your arm. The machine separates your plasma from your red and white blood cells, keeps the plasma and returns the blood cells to your body. Payment is made immediately upon completion of the donation process, which takes up to an hour and a half. You can donate plasma as often as twice a week.

There are over 450 plasma centers across the United States and Europe, and each center sets its own pay rate for donations. To find a facility near you and to learn more about the donation process, visit www.DonatingPlasma.org.

Plasma isn't the only part of your body you can exchange for money. You can also **donate your eggs and sperm** (although obviously not both.) The egg donation process is quite involved and takes eight to ten weeks to complete. If you're approved as a donor, you'll undergo a series of blood tests and sonograms and be injected with hormones to increase your egg production in the weeks leading up to collection day. At the end you'll receive anywhere from $5,000 to $10,000, depending upon the facility you're working with. You'll also have the satisfaction of knowing that you helped another woman experience the blessings of motherhood.

Since it's not nearly as difficult for men to donate sperm as it is for women to donate eggs, the compensation for guys is quite a bit less: $30 to $200 per donation. But according to the California Cryobank Division, prolific sperm donors can earn up to $1,500 a month.[11] That's a nice goal to shoot for, I suppose…

You can also earn money, save money and help humanity by volunteering to be a guinea pig for research into the effectiveness of new drugs, medical devices and experimental treatments. In other words, by **participating in paid clinical trials**. Each trial is conducted by doctors and has its own eligibility constraints. Some require that you have a particular diagnosis such as cancer, obesity, diabetes or high blood pressure, while others are looking for participants who are healthy so they can be observed and compared to ill participants. Generally speaking, the longer and riskier the trial, the more it pays. Short, simple trials that don't require much of your time and don't have many adverse side effects pay much less. Participating in trials can save you money since you won't have to pay for the medications or treatments that are included in the trial.

If you'd like to receive email notifications of new clinical trials being conducted in your area, visit www. CenterWatch.com/clinical-trials/pns and sign up for their free patient notification service.

---

11   http://www.spermbank.com/why-donate/sperm-donor-pay, accessed July 21, 2016.

If you live near a research university, check its website for a database of **psychological studies** they're conducting. Studies about sleep, learning, communication, personality, child development, mood, etc. are always in need of participants. I just did a quick check of a small U.S. university's psychology department website and found six such studies at that institution alone. Each pays $40 or $50 to do simple things like filling out a questionnaire or playing a game/doing an activity with the researchers. Fun, interesting, meaningful gigs that earn money, too? Sign me up!

Participating in Paid Focus Groups

Market research is a HUGE business in the world today. Companies want to know exactly what consumers are thinking and how best to reach them, so they hire firms to conduct "focus groups" to tell them just that. A focus group is a specially selected set of consumers who are surveyed or taken through a discussion process by a professional group leader to determine their thoughts about a particular brand, product, service, political candidate, television program, etc. Some groups meet in person and others are queried online. The people chosen for each group will match the demographic the company is targeting... say, a brewery might want a group consisting of single men between the ages of 18 and 35 who regularly drink beer, or a manufacturer of ferret food would only want people who have ferrets. The group will be asked for their attitudes and beliefs about the brand in question. At the end of the session the firm conducting the focus group reports the findings to the company and also pays the group participants for their time, ranging anywhere from $75 to several hundred dollars.

If you'd like to be considered for inclusion in focus groups, you can register online with the firms that conduct them. Two of the most popular ones are AdvancedFocus.com and FocusRoom. com. You'll create a profile with your age, sex, location, race, marital status, education level, household income, etc. and then wait to be contacted. There is no guarantee that you'll ever hear from these firms, but your odds increase if you register with more than one of them.

Entertain Strangers

You can make money becoming a "local host" and renting a room or your entire home through AirBnB.com, which calls itself the "worldwide accommodations leader." With more than two million listings in 30,000 cities around the globe, AirBnB is not only helping hosts make money but also helping travelers find the perfect place to rest their weary heads.

To cash in on the AirBnB phenomenon, you'll create a free profile on their site with your location, how many rooms you want to rent and whether they'll be private or shared rooms, how many people you're willing to accommodate, and how much you want to charge. The site helps you come up with that amount by giving you the average rate for your locale. You indicate how involved you intend to be with your renters (will you meet and greet them upon arrival? Will you be serving them breakfast? Will you be staying on-site or off? Can you provide concierge services or transportation?) Then you'll describe the accommodations, enter the dates they're available, and upload photos to finish your property's listing, which will be visible to anyone looking for accommodations in your area. If someone chooses to rent your property, AirBnB will notify you and you will communicate directly with the guest to arrange their stay. Guests pay you through AirBnB, which keeps three percent of the rental fee. In exchange, AirBnB provides you with the listing on their website plus insurance to cover any property damage or liability claims should someone get hurt.

The amount you earn via AirBnB depends on your location, your property's attributes and how often you rent. It's an especially good option for people who live in a high tourist area or have a second home in one. Check it out and see what you think.

◆

Opportunity Snapshot: Unconventional Money-Makers

Pros: Free to get started; interesting, meaningful ways to make money; pay can be good

Cons: Participation in some tasks can be uncomfortable and time consuming.

Best Fit For: People with an entrepreneurial spirit; those who enjoy meeting other people; those who are not squeamish about medical procedures

Tech Savvy Scale: 2—some tasks require use of a computer, digital camera, and the ability to navigate websites

◆

Further Exploration:

- For a database of hundreds of clinical trials that are currently looking for participants, visit www.ClinicalTrials.gov.
- Another platform for renting to vacationers is "Vacation Rentals By Owner" at www.VRBO.com.

CONCLUSION

I don't know about you, but I've lost count of all the money-making opportunities we've explored in the previous chapters. My goal has been to show you that there are limitless opportunities out there for you, and to inspire you to try a few of them for yourself. I hope I've achieved that objective.

Whether it's operating as a self-employed chauffeur, selling your crafts online, setting up a booth at a flea market, writing freelance articles, engaging in some crowd working, offering your services through one of the many various web-based platforms, doing affiliate marketing on your blog, taking online surveys, renting your guest room to a tourist... the fun is in using today's technology and discovering your right fit. One of these ideas may strike you as a clear winner and that's all you'll ever need. Or perhaps you'll decide to piece together three or four different activities and do each one for a couple of hours every week as an experiment to find out what works best.

The point is that there is no right or wrong way to do this. The ideas I've presented here are intended to get your creative juices flowing and show you how other people like you have been able to make extra money. So even though we've made it to the end of this book, it's really only the beginning of what

I hope will be a fun and lucrative discovery process for you. Because remember: just as every additional dollar you bring in enriches your bank account, so does every additional bit of new knowledge enrich your life. I sincerely hope the information contained in this book has made you feel a little richer today.

Good luck, and Happy Earning!

ABOUT THE AUTHOR

Mike Zechmann grew up in South Georgia in a small town called Waycross, where he learned the value of a dollar and the satisfaction of an honest day's work by giving alligator boat tours through the Okefenokee Swamp each summer as a teen. After high school graduation, Mike moved to Baltimore, Maryland to attend  the Johns Hopkins University with the goal of becoming a surgeon. He quickly changed his major to Applied Mathematics and Statistics (with a minor in Entrepreneurship) because he was good with numbers and enjoyed working with them. He earned his degree in only three years and immediately started working in the financial services industry, where he remains to this day.

An avid tennis player, Mike met his wife, Rebeca, while playing club tennis during his college years at Johns Hopkins. The couple lives outside Baltimore with their two beautiful daughters, Catherine and Madeline. Mike continues to play in

USTA tennis leagues around Maryland and also enjoys outdoor physical activities such as golf, running, skiing, biking, hiking, spending time on the beach, and attending sporting events. He's a huge Minnesota Vikings fan, and frankly he's as baffled by that fact as everyone else.

Morgan James
Speakers Group

↗ www.TheMorganJamesSpeakersGroup.com

We connect Morgan James published
authors with live and online events
and audiences who will benefit
from their expertise.